How to Travel on a Budget

How to plan affordable travel, make the cheapest trip itinerary, and book discounted accommodations.

GEORGE LAAS

ISBN: 9798623368324

Table of Contents

Introduction

Nowadays, traveling around the world is not considered to be rare and expensive. Almost everyone can afford to visit other cities and even countries. And with the ability to work remotely, some people spend most of their lives traveling. It has become a core part of their lifestyle.

The purpose of this book is to help you plan trips. You will not find here any information about insurance, things that you need to take with you on the journey, which bank cards to use, etc. The book aims to help you choose the perfect route and plan your budget based on it. Therefore, the main focus will be on logistics (to be more precise, ways of reaching your destination), and lodging in the chosen location.

I will not offer you trips that cost only $20, $30, or $50 per day. I will not do this for one reason: the standard of living in different countries and even cities within one country can vary greatly. For example, in some regions of India, $20 is more than enough for a comfortable stay (lodging, food, and leisure/tourism), but if you decide to fly to the Maldives, which are geographically closer, this sum of money will not be enough. For this reason, my goal is to show you how to find and plan a trip for cheaper than average for your desired location.

Also, I would like to add that, in this book, I will not consider free housing options through platforms such as CouchSurfing, or hostels, where you will be packed like sardines. But I will make sure that it is a private room with easy access to a bathroom and a kitchen.

Examples of Travel Routes

First, I would like to show you some simple examples of previously planned trips.

Example 1. A trip for two people from New York to Punta Cana.

Duration of the trip: March 2 – March 18.

There is a non-stop round-trip flight available from the John F. Kennedy International Airport that costs $325 per person. Also, I have found an attractive housing option in one of the most prestigious areas - Bavaro. A one-bedroom apartment for two with a kitchen, washing machine, bathroom, Wi-Fi and a patio, which costs only $332.

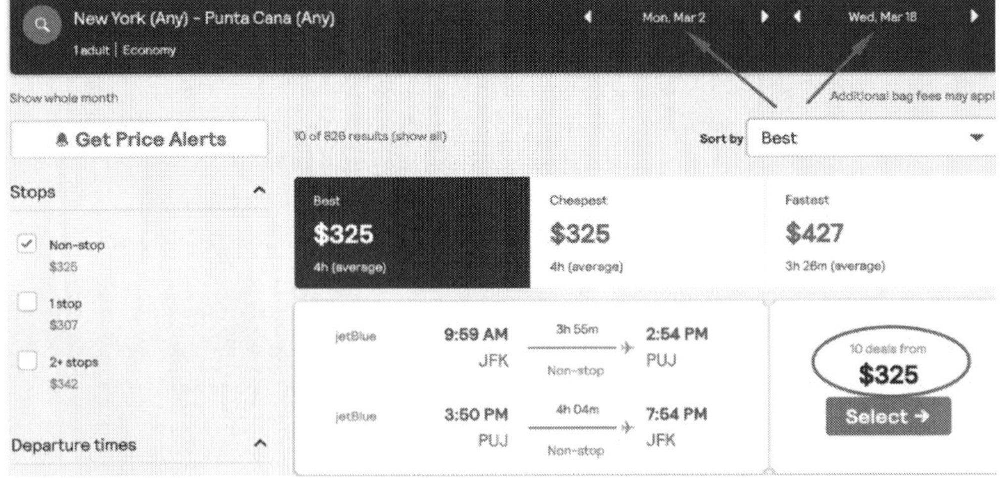

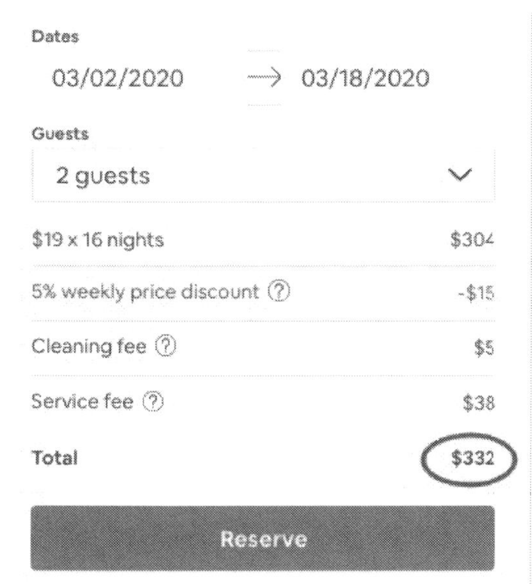

So, you will need to pay for everything 2*325(ticket price) + 332 (housing) = $982, which equals to $491 per person.

Example 2. A Boston – Puerto Rico short trip (7 days) for two people.

Duration of the trip: February 24 – March 4.

The flight ticket costs $134 per person.

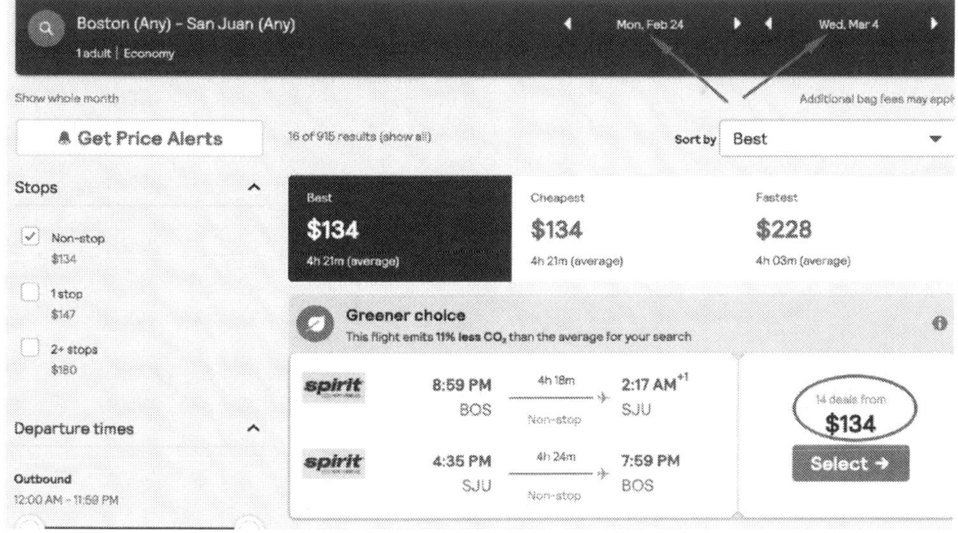

Housing costs $291 per two people. So, the total will be 134*2+291= $559, or to be more precise, 559/2= $279,50 per person.

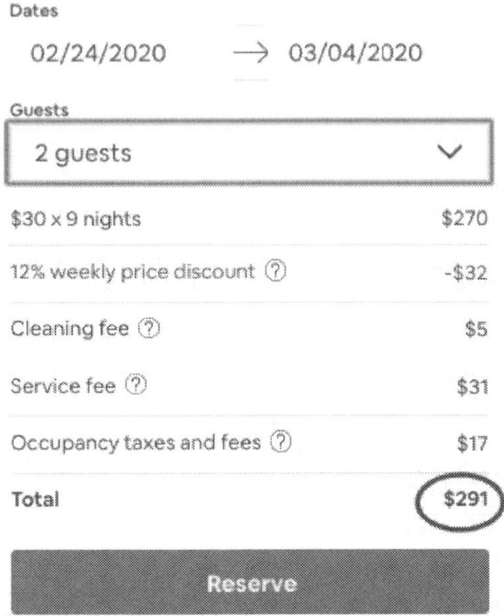

Example 3. A three week trip from London to Spain (Valencia, Barcelona, Alicante) for two people.

Duration of the trip: February 11 – March 3.

The tickets for the London-Barcelona flight on February 11 costs £9 per person.

A nice apartment in Barcelona for seven days costs £233.

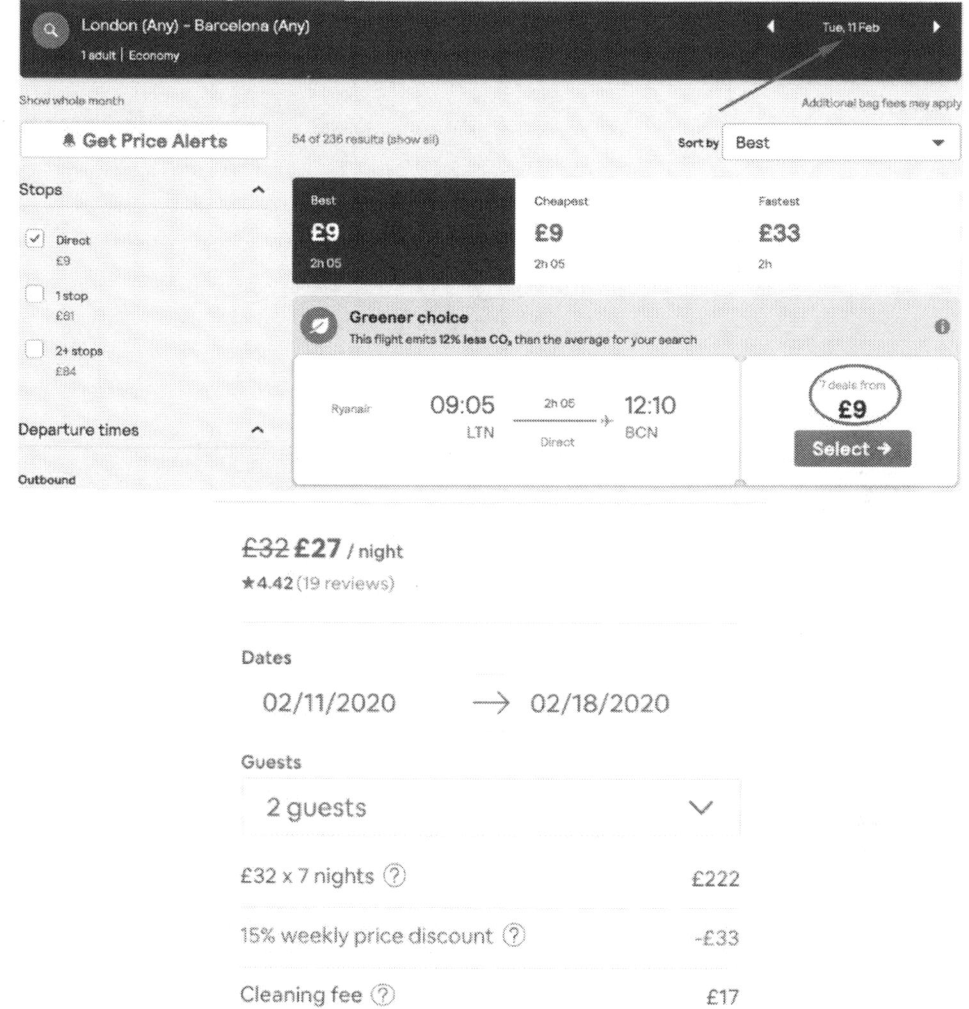

A bus ticket from Barcelona to Valencia costs €5 (£4.25). An apartment in Valencia for seven days costs £203.

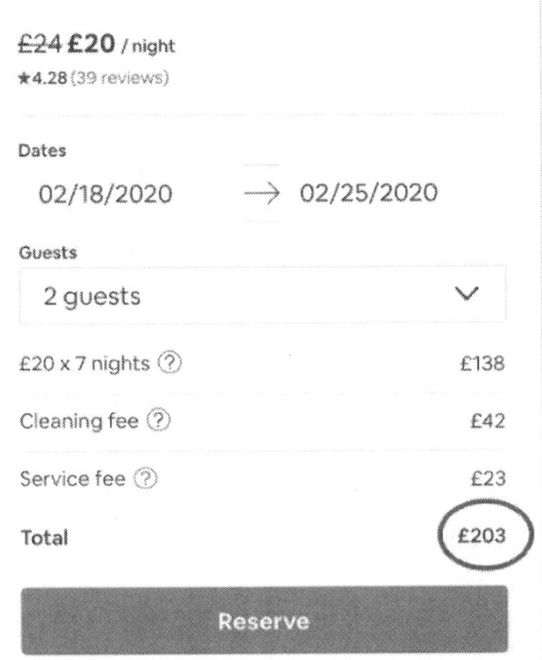

Next, you will need to take the Alsa bus to Alicante. The price of the ticket is €5,35 (£4.55). An apartment in Alicante costs £148.

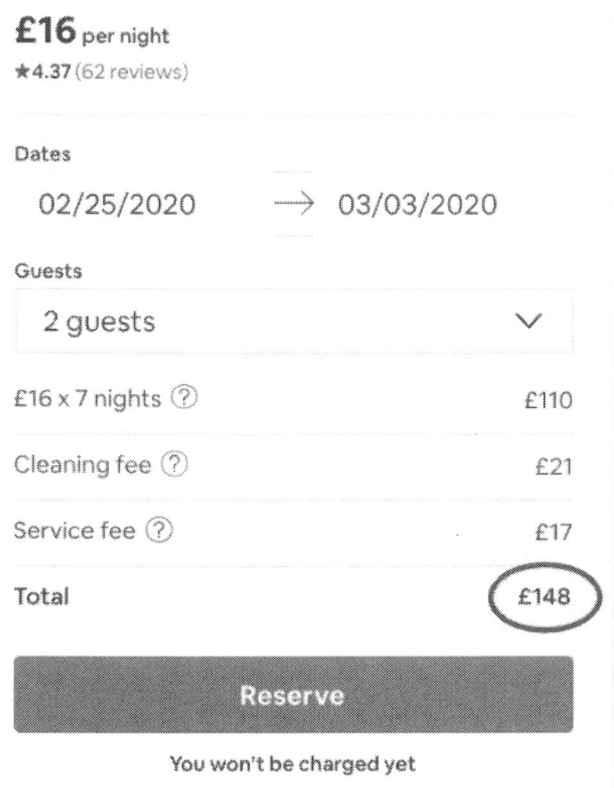

At the end of your trip, you will have to take one more flight, which will be from Alicante to London and costs £13.

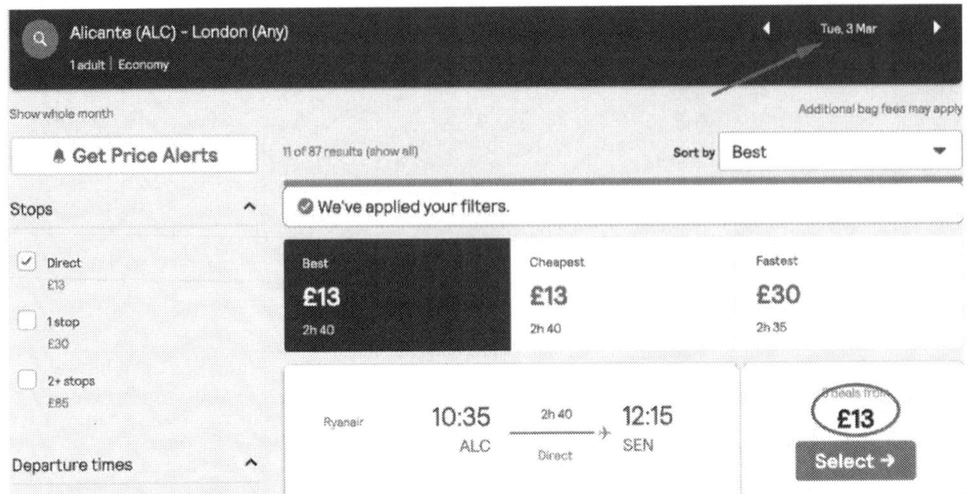

So, we get the total of 9*2+233+4,25*2+203+4,55*2+148+13*2= £645,6. The trip will cost 645,6/2=£322,8 per person.

These examples include only prices. I didn't show you where they came from. **If you want to know more, please read on.** Later in the book, I will explain in detail how to choose the best and most suitable tickets and housing options.

Route Search Options

There are a couple of possible cases. The method that we choose to plan the best budget-friendly trip is based on the case that it corresponds to.

The first case — when you know where you want to go and when. In this case, the planning process will simply be finding the best suitable route from Place A to Place B at a chosen time. The only thing that can be changed here is the sequence in which you visit the selected places if there are more than two. Also, in this case, there will not be many suitable routes to choose from.

The second case — when you know the exact place that you want to visit but haven't chosen the dates. This case is more flexible. You will get more options than in the first case.

The third case — when you have no idea where you want to go but have already selected the dates. In this case, you will have even more options, as there are multiple travel destinations to choose from.

The fourth case — when you do not know where you want to go and have not selected the dates yet. In this case, you will get plenty of options.

Now, let's look at the trip options that we get for each case. We will start with the last one, the fourth case, as it is the easiest to find and end with the first one.

Choosing a Travel Destination

As previously mentioned, we begin with the case when the final destination and the trip dates are unknown. Usually, the main sources of expenses are transportation — the type of transport that you use from the beginning to the end of your trip — and, of course, the lodging expenses.

This is only the beginning of our planning process. The next step is to give good thought into choosing a travel destination. Only after this crucial step will we be able to start planning the trip.

Type of Transport

As a rule, I begin the trip planning with logistics — and only after I look for a suitable lodging option. In cases when you find some super-cheap lodging options, you can do it the other way around. For example, when I am planning for a summer vacation by the sea in Europe, I first look up the prices of lodging options and only then will I choose the type of transport.

Flights

Now, most people choose to travel by plane. If it doesn't matter for you which city you fly from, use a platform that will help you find the cheapest flights from your desired airport or country. I prefer to use Skyscanner. It has the most user-friendly interface and is free.

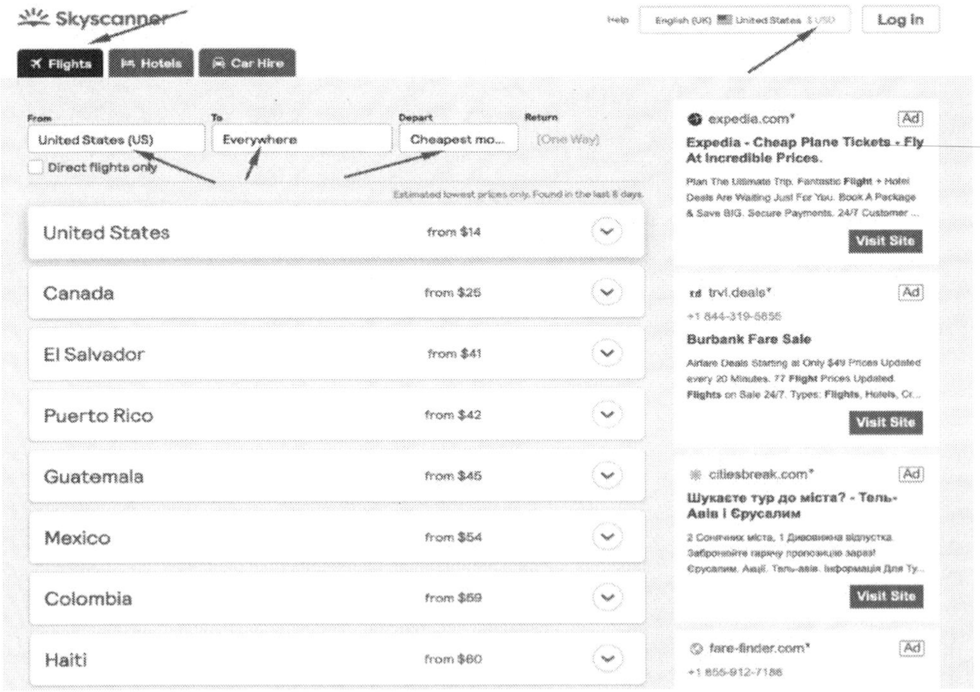

This is an example of how to find the cheapest tickets for flights departing from the United States.

1. In the "From" box, select the desired airport or country.
2. In the "To" box, select the final destination. Since we don't know the final destination, select "Everywhere."
3. In the "Depart" box, select the date. In this case, select "Cheapest month."

The cheapest flights are the domestic ones, at $14, followed by Canada and El Salvador ($25 and $41, respectively).

Europe has many cheap airlines, or as they are also called: low-cost airlines.

A list of low-cost airlines you can find in Appendix 1 at the end of the book.

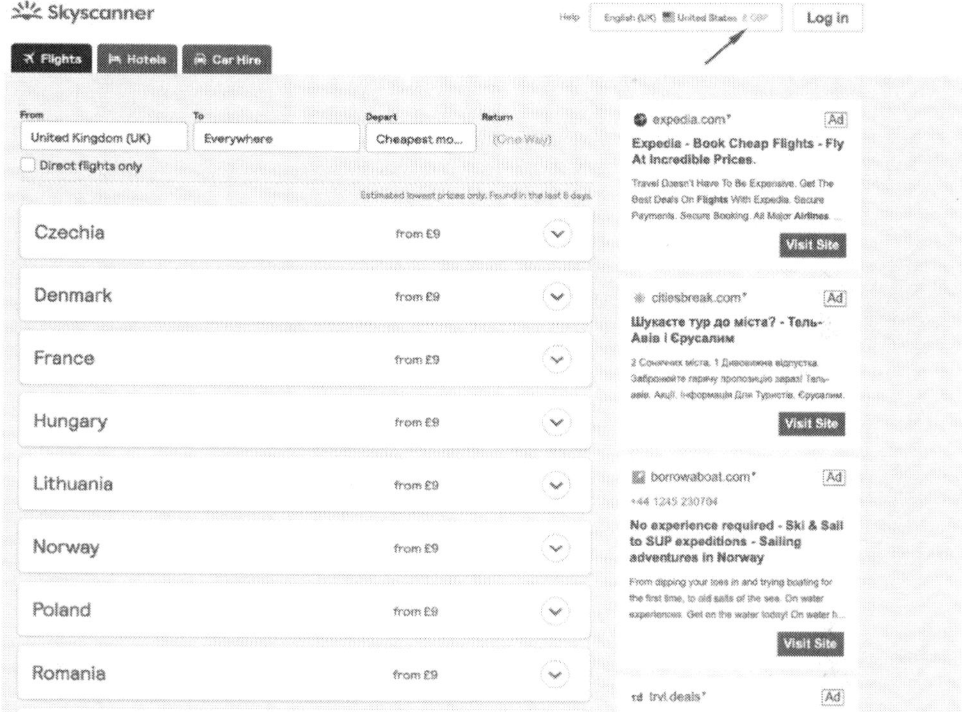

If you look for flights departing from the United Kingdom, you will find some that cost only £9. For this price, you can fly to the Czech Republic, Denmark, France, Hungary, Lithuania, Norway, Poland, and Romania.

This kind of search is the simplest one, and in the following examples, we will get into more complicated ones.

Now let's see what options we get if we choose a specific destination point and a particular date. To do this, you should type the destination and date in the "To" and "Depart" boxes.

But first, let's consider the option when we know the destination point and haven't chosen the dates yet.

Check out the pictures below. Let's look for a flight from the U.S. to London. As you can see, if you choose to depart from Los Angeles, you will be able to get there for $135 on the following days of March 2020: 9, 29, 30. So, you can see that there are many options, and if one date doesn't work for you, then you can choose a different one.

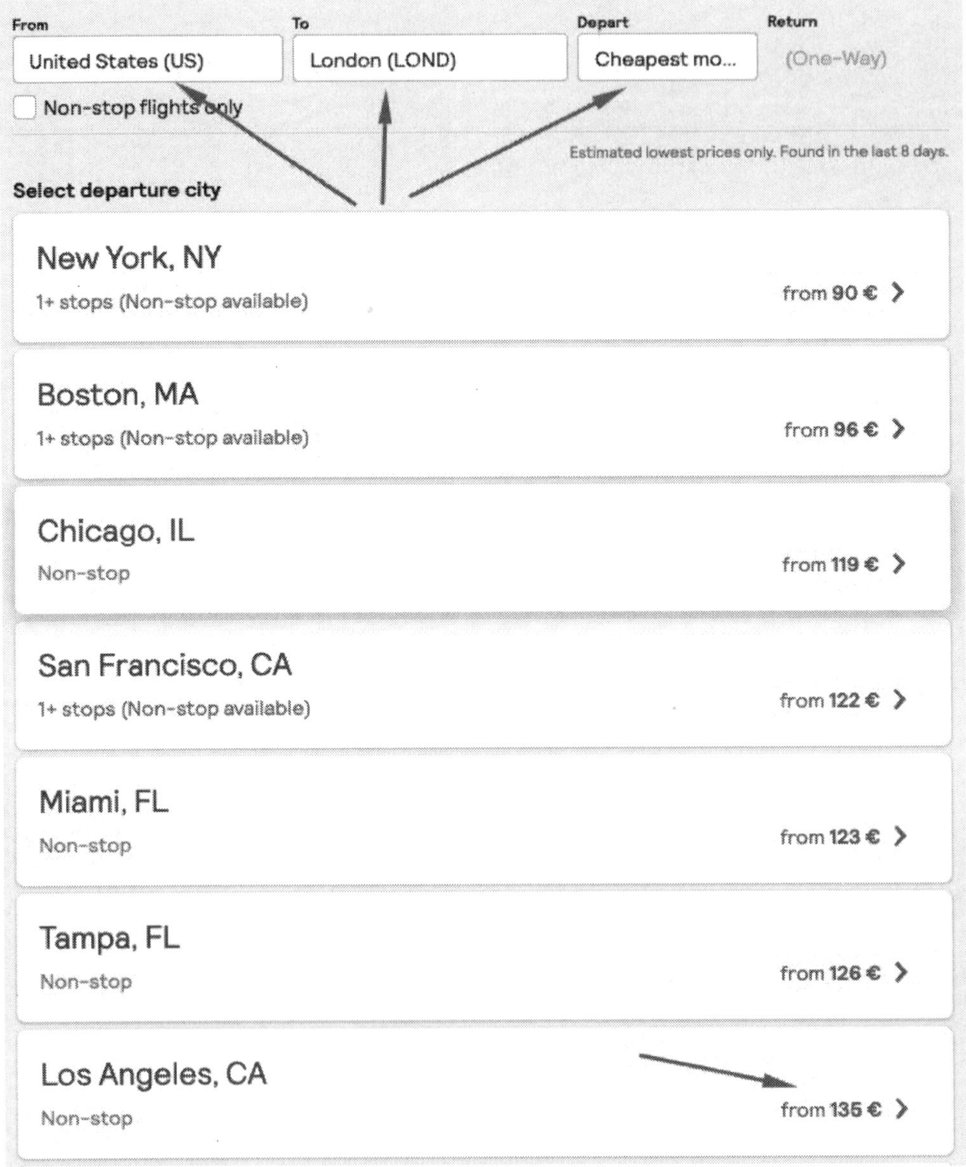

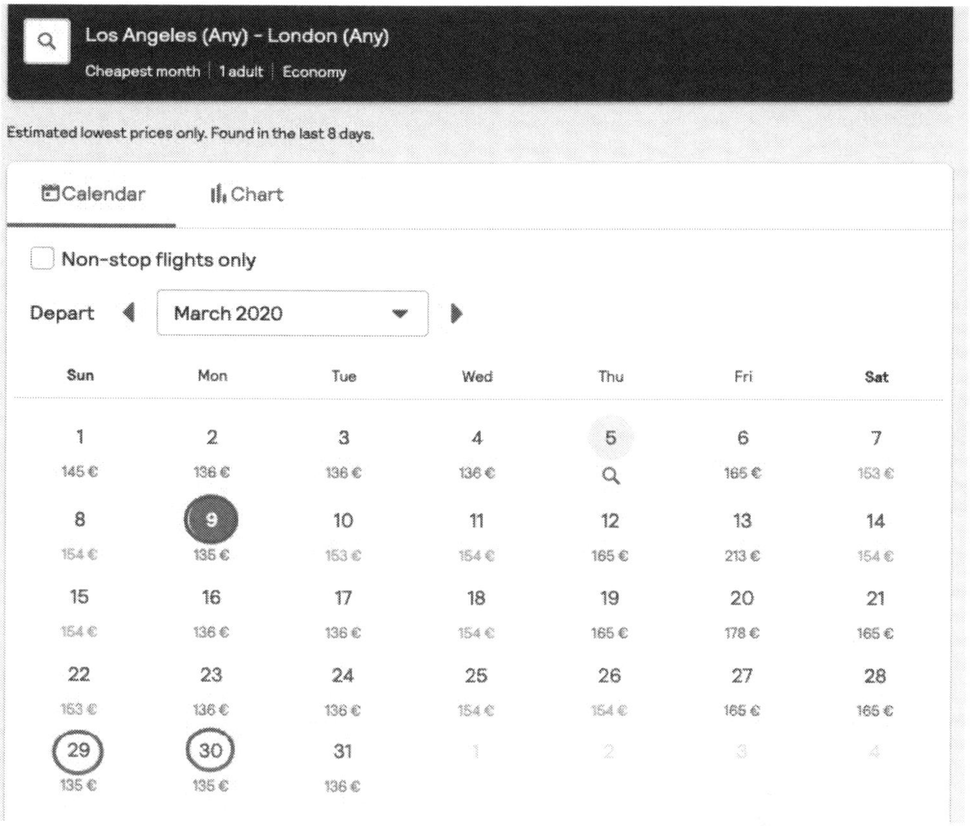

Los Angeles (Any) - London (Any)

Cheapest month | 1 adult | Economy

Estimated lowest prices only. Found in the last 8 days.

Calendar | Chart

Non-stop flights only

Depart March 2020

Sun	Mon	Tue	Wed	Thu	Fri	Sat
1 145 €	2 136 €	3 136 €	4 136 €	5	6 165 €	7 153 €
8 154 €	9 135 €	10 153 €	11 154 €	12 165 €	13 213 €	14 154 €
15 154 €	16 136 €	17 136 €	18 154 €	19 165 €	20 178 €	21 165 €
22 153 €	23 136 €	24 136 €	25 154 €	26 154 €	27 165 €	28 165 €
29 135 €	30 135 €	31 136 €	1	2	3	4

Now let's look at what the platform has for us if we know the date, but have no idea where we want to go.

Imagine that you want to travel somewhere on your Christmas vacation. In the "Depart" box, select a date that comes a few days before Christmas, like, for example, December 22, and take a look at the countries that you may be interested in.

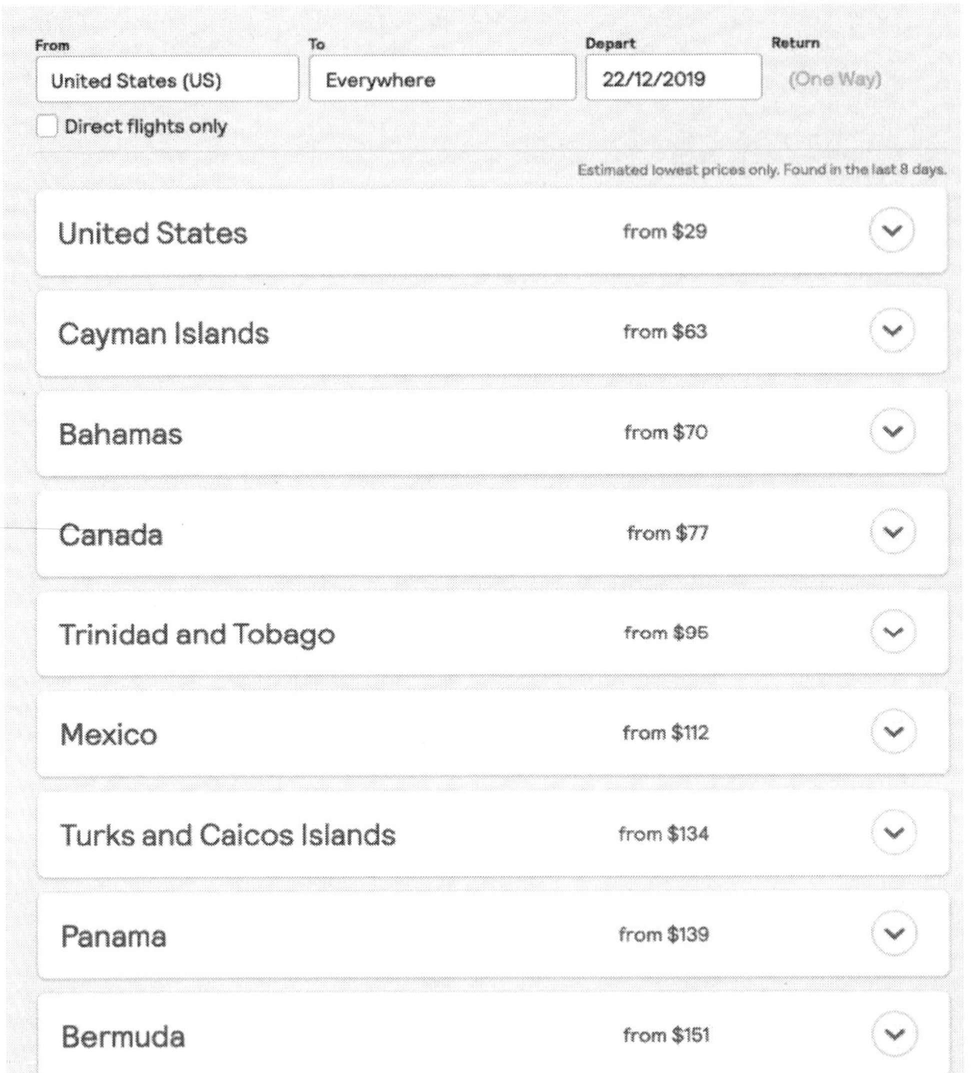

If you choose the price range of up to $150, then you will see that there are plenty of one-way flight options — the Cayman Islands, Bahamas, Trinidad and Tobago, Mexico, Panama, etc.

As you can see, the previous two examples gave us various options that were $150 and under, and we also could choose the destination or the date. With the first example, you can get pretty cheap offers, even up to $50, along with the opportunity to choose between the options.

And now, let's take a look at the case when we already know the destination country and dates. To make a better comparison, in the "Depart" box, type in the 22nd of December, and the "To" box type in London.

It turns out that the cheapest flight departs from Orlando and costs $326. But if you need to fly from New York, for example, then it will cost you $469.

And there are no other options for us. That is why this kind of search has the least number of options and is the most expensive one.

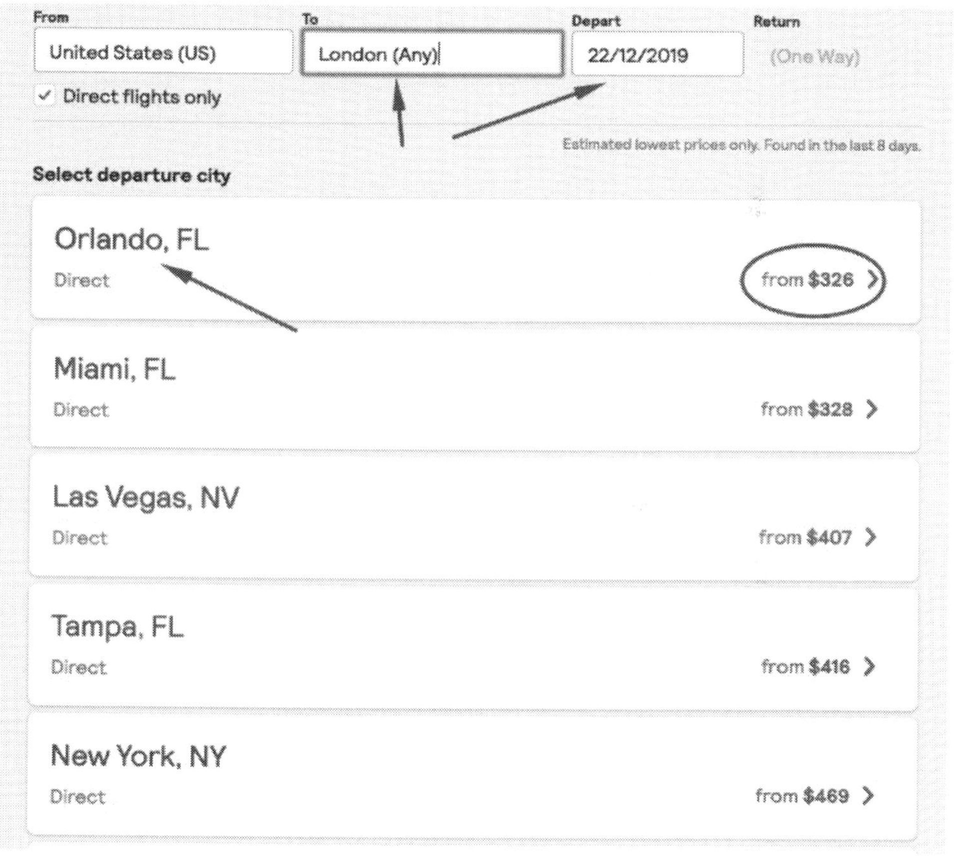

Layovers

Now, instead of considering only direct flights, let's find the option of taking a trip with one or more layovers. The stops can be long or short, but Skyscanner takes into account the short ones and creates a route based on them. To do this, you'll need to uncheck the "Direct flights only" option below the search box.

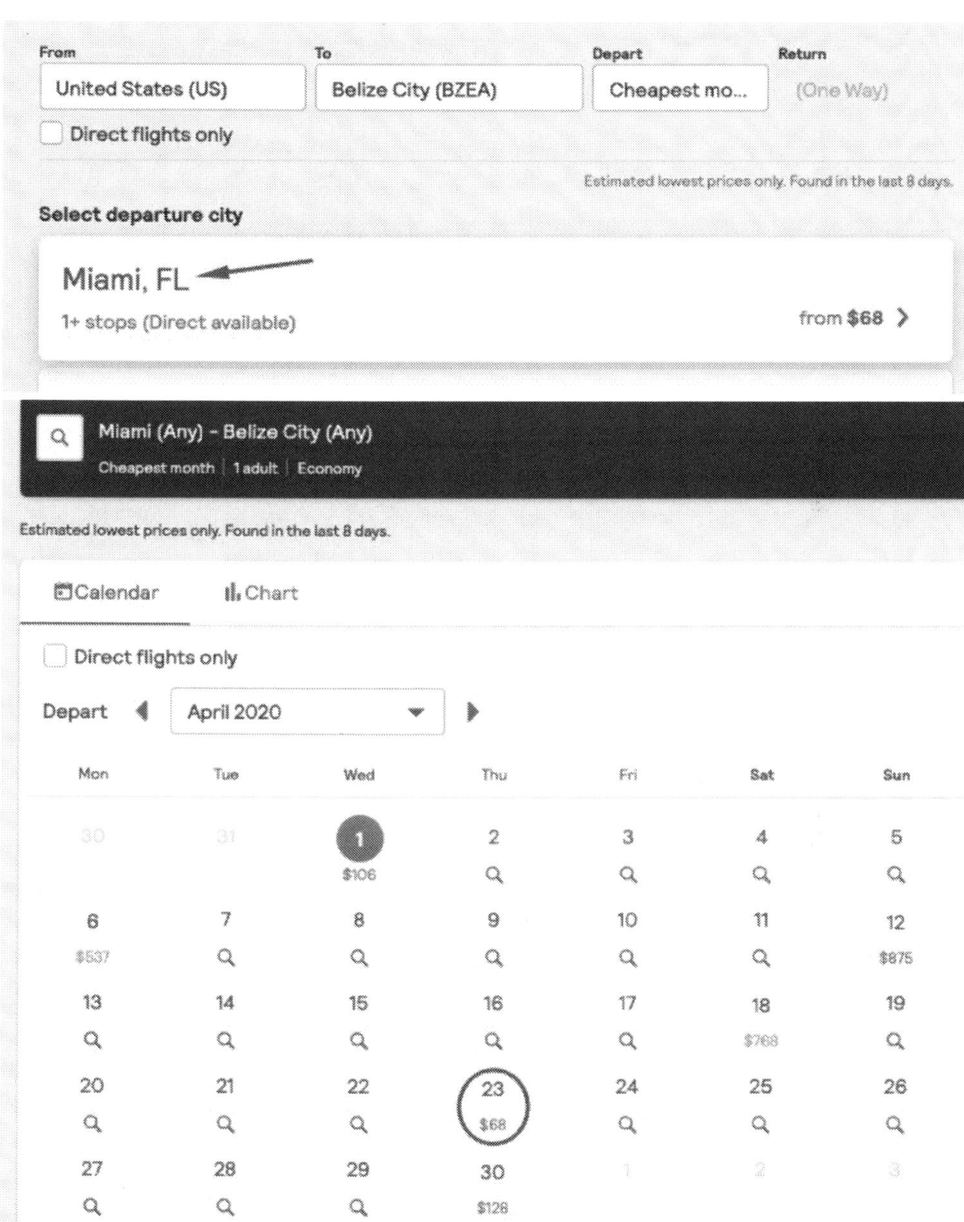
From
United States (US)
To
Belize City (BZEA)
Depart
Cheapest mo...
Return
(One Way)
Direct flights only
Estimated lowest prices only. Found in the last 8 days.
Select departure city
Miami, FL
1+ stops (Direct available)
from $68
Miami (Any) - Belize City (Any)
Cheapest month | 1 adult | Economy
Estimated lowest prices only. Found in the last 8 days.
Calendar
Chart
Direct flights only
Depart
April 2020
Mon Tue Wed Thu Fri Sat Sun
30 31 1 2 3 4 5
$106
6 7 8 9 10 11 12
$537 $875
13 14 15 16 17 18 19
$768
20 21 22 23 24 25 26
$68
27 28 29 30 1 2 3
$128

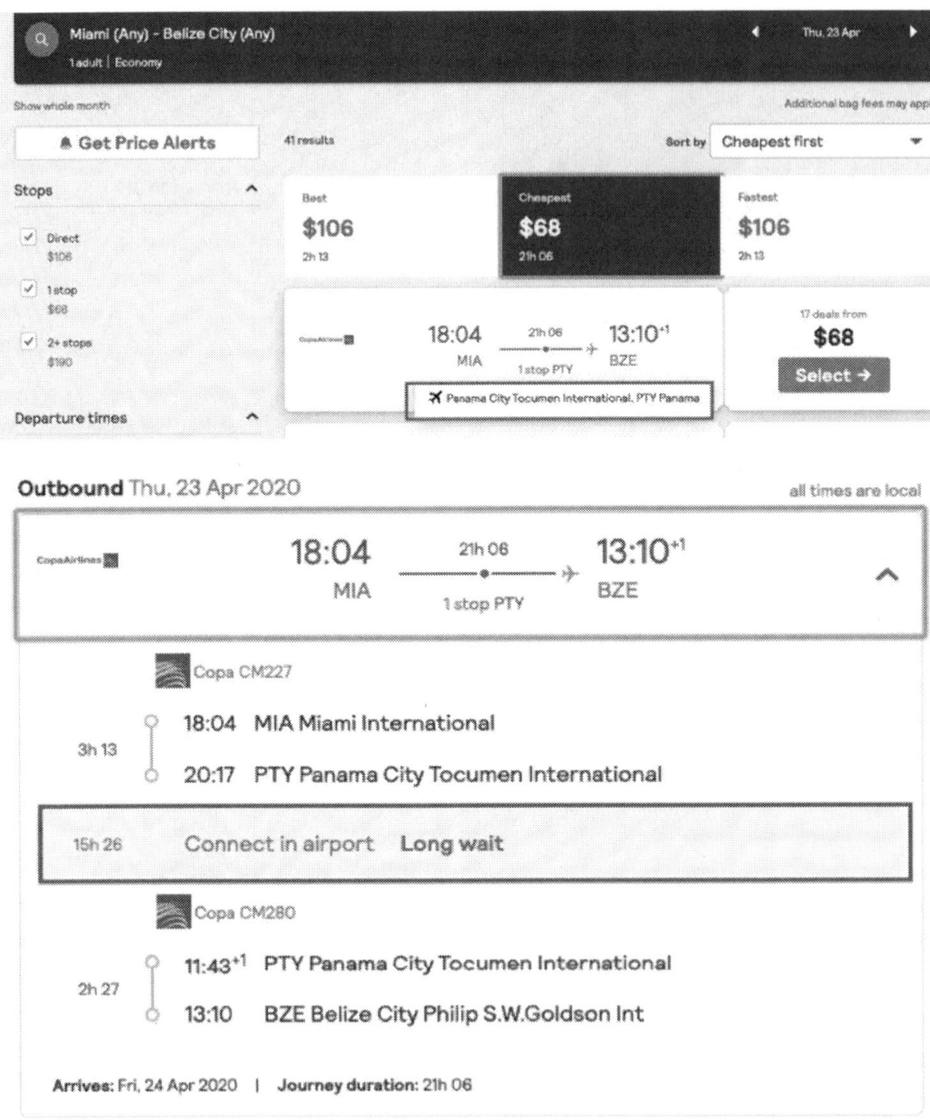

For example, there is an available flight on April 23, departing from the USA (Miami) to Belize with one layover in Panama that will be 15 hours and 26 minutes long. Of course, spending 15 hours in an airport is not exactly an ideal layover. That is why our task will be to find options that will minimize the waiting time. But I do not recommend a waiting period of fewer than 3 hours. Boarding usually begins 2 hours before departure, and given that flights get delayed sometimes, it is good to have that one extra hour.

Now, let's consider the options where we can use layovers to our advantage. The first of such cases is a long layover. If the arrival date is not so important when you're traveling, you can use the stopover to visit another city and even stay there for a day, or a couple of days.

What are the benefits of doing so? Firstly, you will have time to explore and do something fun in the new place. Secondly, it may turn out that the flight from the layover airport to your previously chosen destination will be cheaper the next day or a few days later. In such cases, the layover should be at least 24 hours long, or even a couple of days long. Unfortunately, you will not be able to automatically track such lengthy stops with the help of online services.

Therefore, you will need to look for options manually. Take a look at the following example.

Let's say you are traveling from New York to Tenerife, but with a layover at Dublin. And you are going on this trip on February 14. First, let's take a look at the possibility of a short stopover. We aim to find the cheapest flights for the whole New York – Dublin – Tenerife journey.

The best possible option for the New York – Dublin flight costs $312. However, make sure to pay attention to the time of arrival, which is at 04:45 a.m. on February 15.

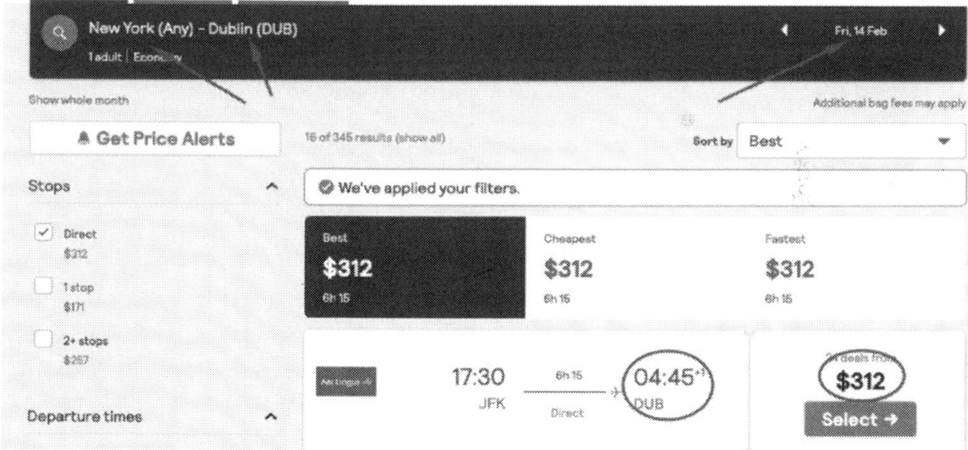

Now let's look at the options that we have for the Dublin – Tenerife flight. A flight operated by Ryanair Airlines departs at 8:25 a.m. on February 15. So, the waiting time in Dublin will be 3 hours and 40 minutes, which is a nice and short layover. The entire trip will cost us $312 + $271 = $583.

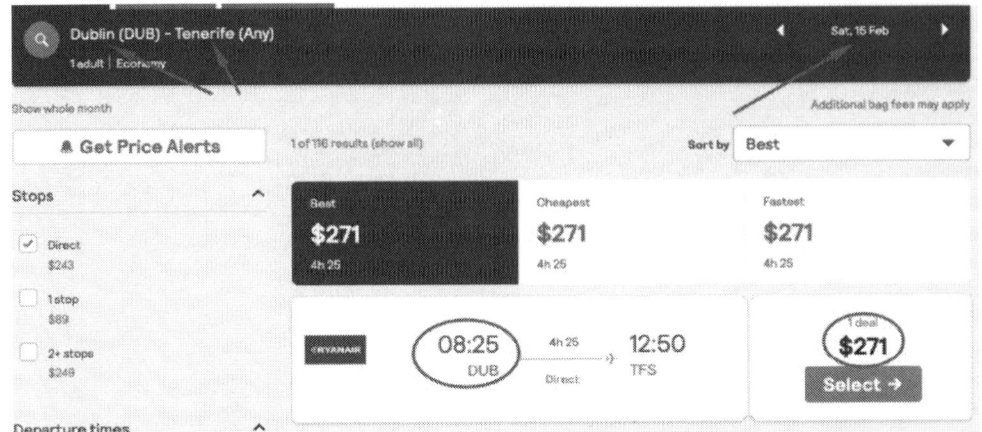

Let's also consider the option of staying in Dublin for a whole day. If you have never visited Dublin, you might be happy to have some time to walk around the city and see the sights. And the Dublin – Tenerife flight will be not on February 15, but on February 16.

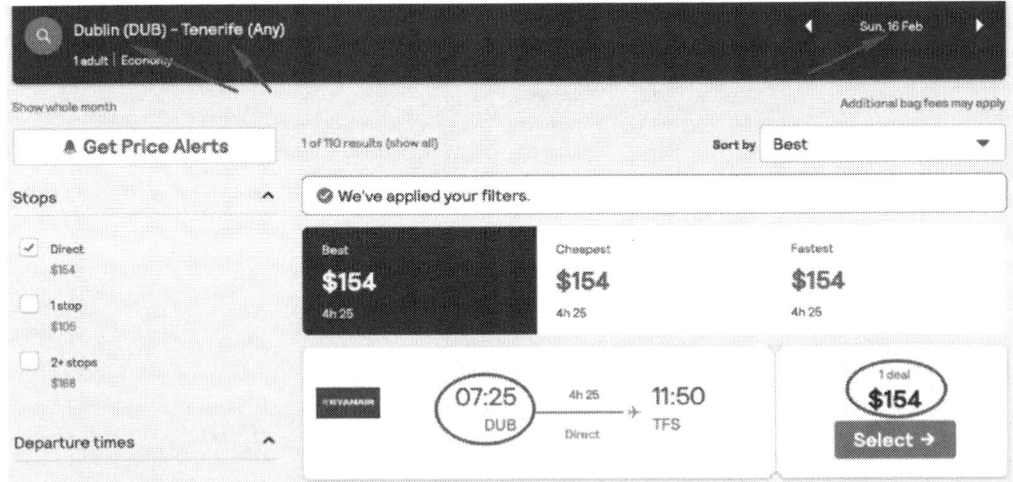

As it turns out, on February 16, the price of the ticket is not $271, but $154. So, if we make a layover in Dublin, the total cost of the trip will be $312 + $154 = $466, which makes it $117 cheaper. You can use the saved money to rent an apartment, have a tasty meal, and go sightseeing, and you'll still have some money left.

But a logical question comes up: what if you choose to fly to Dublin not on February 14, but on February 15, and then hop on the Ryanair flight at 7:25 a.m. on February 16, on the one that costs $154? We looked up those dates, but it turned out that there are no cheap flights from New York to Dublin on the 15th. Moreover, the time of arrival and departure isn't convenient, meaning that there is not at least a 3-hour gap between them.

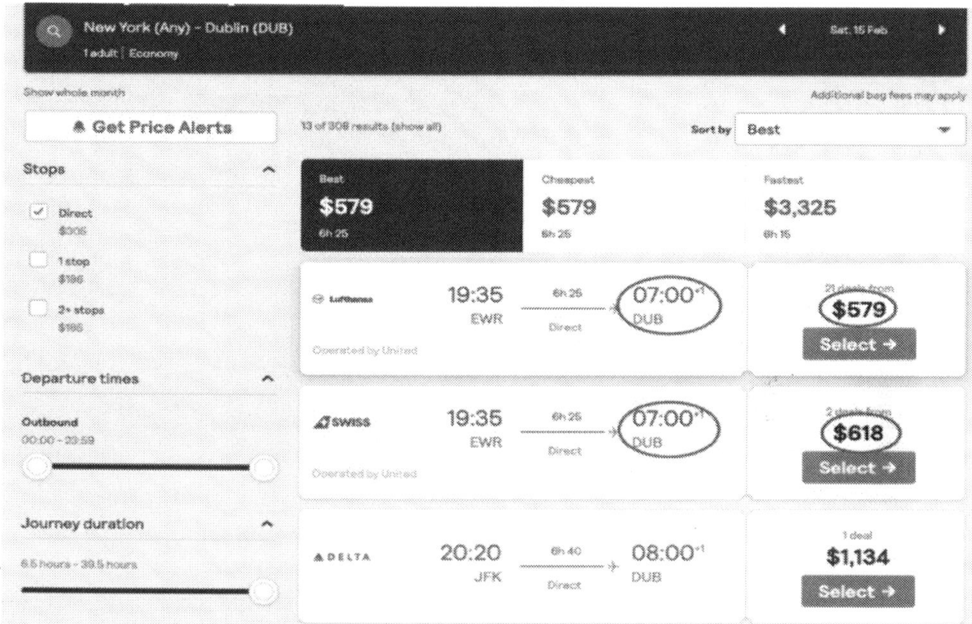

I want to clarify that I did not choose the best possible New York – Tenerife flight option, as there are other options, ones that have layovers not in Dublin, but in other countries, which can be better and cheaper. But the point of this example was to show you how the search for the best route can be conducted and that the automatic search on the flight-finding platforms will not show you all of the available options, especially in the case of a long layover.

Now we will have a look at a more complicated search of possible flight options with layovers. To be more precise, we will search for such flights that require a transfer to another airport. Quite often, especially in Europe, it happens that when two airports are close to each other, there is a possibility of getting from one airport to the other for an insignificant price by some direct transport or through the city. A great example of such airports in Vienna and Bratislava, and Copenhagen and Malmo. And if you use their bus transfer service, then getting to the other airport will be cheap.

Let's imagine that on December 26, you need to get from Dublin to Catania (Sicily, Italy). There are no direct flights, which is why there will be a layover. If you use the automatic search on Skyscanner, you will see that the cheapest flight costs €214 and that the layover will be in Rome.

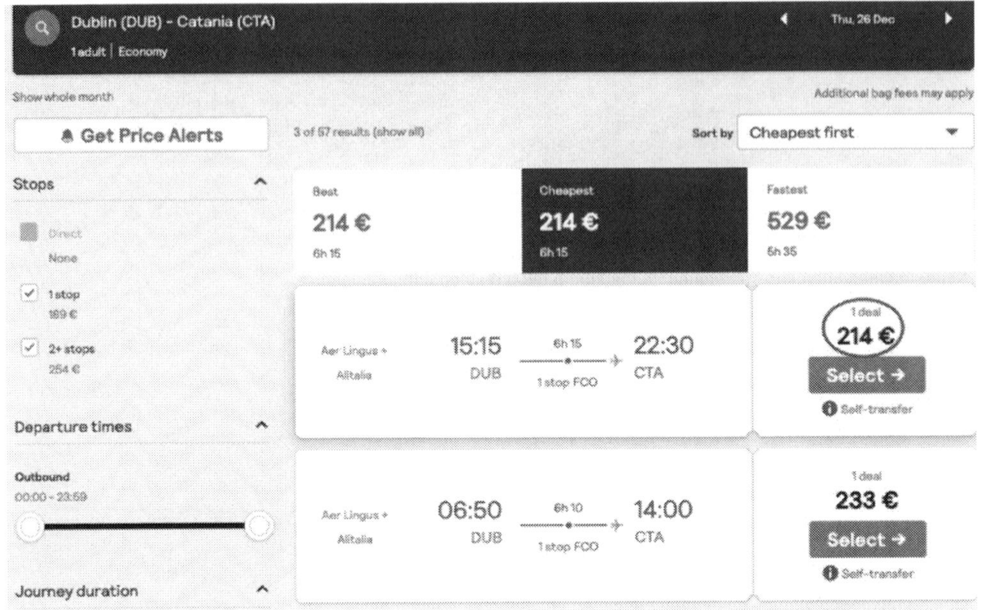

Let's see what happens if we search manually. And the search shows us that there can be a layover in Bratislava (Slovakia). So, the Dublin – Bratislava flight costs €84.99, and Bratislava – Catania, €139.98.

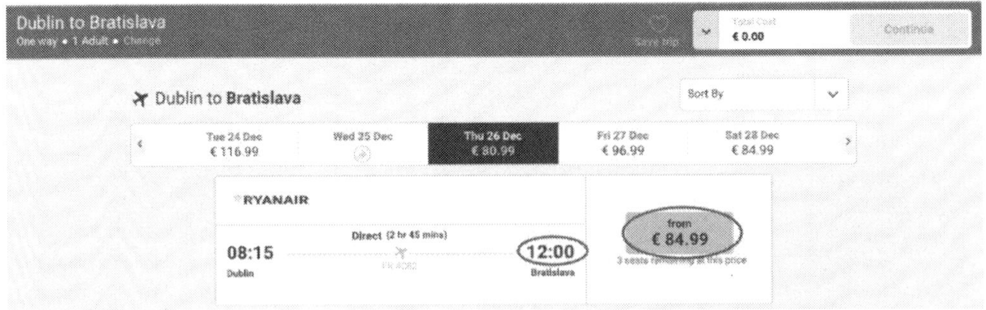

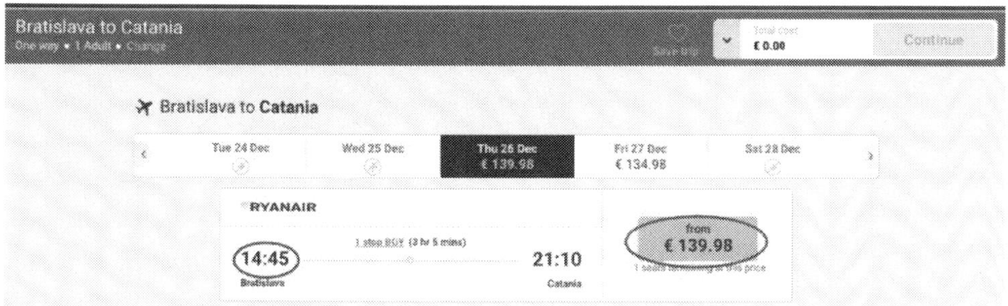

If we add up the prices for the two flights (€84.99 + €139.98), we will get a sum of €224.97. This option is not as good as the one that Skyscanner found for us. Moreover, the layover is only two hours and 45 minutes long, which is a bit risky, as it is less than 3 hours. And there will also be one more layover in Bergamo.

But if you transfer from the Bratislava airport to Vienna airport, which will cost you only €6.99, and hop on the Vienna – Catania flight, which costs €79.99, the total of the whole trip will be €84.99 + €79.99 + €6.99 = €171.97. And if you have the Wizz Discount Club program activated (I'll tell you all about it later), the trip will cost only €161.97. Besides, the departure time from Vienna airport is more convenient — 17:10.

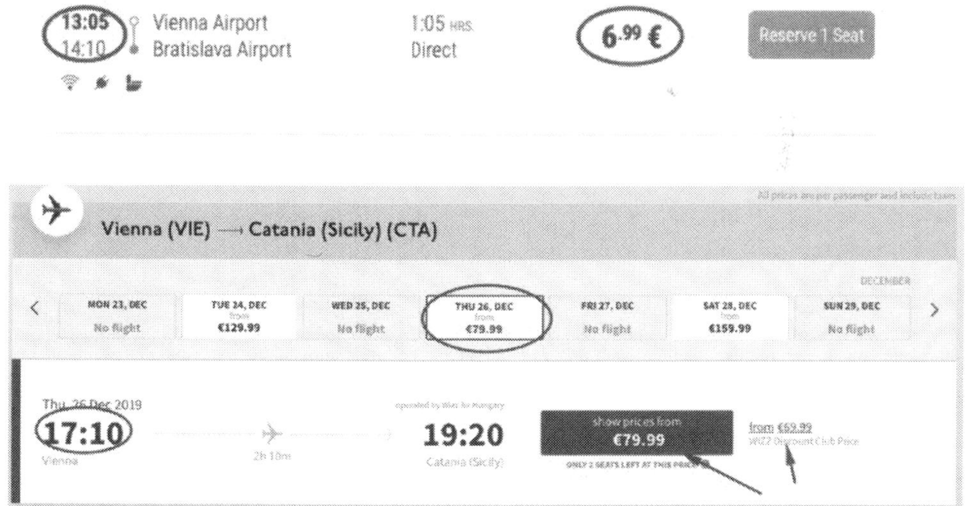

As you can see above, transferring to a nearby airport and flying from there allows you to reduce the cost by €214 – €171.97 = €42.03 (with the Wizz Discount Club program: €52.03).

Airline Rewards Programs

I will not give you a description of airline rewards programs in this section, as you can find such information almost on every Internet blog. Plus, the process of acquiring such rewards is pretty standard — after you travel some distance with a certain airline, you receive miles/bonuses for it and can use them to pay for the next flight. It seems to me that on the official website of any airline, you can find all of the details regarding their loyalty programs.

That is why I will draw your attention to such airline rewards programs that require you to buy a membership. Usually, such programs are used by European low-cost airlines like WizzAir and Volotea. The point of such programs is that you pay an annual membership fee, and they give you discounts on tickets, baggage, etc.

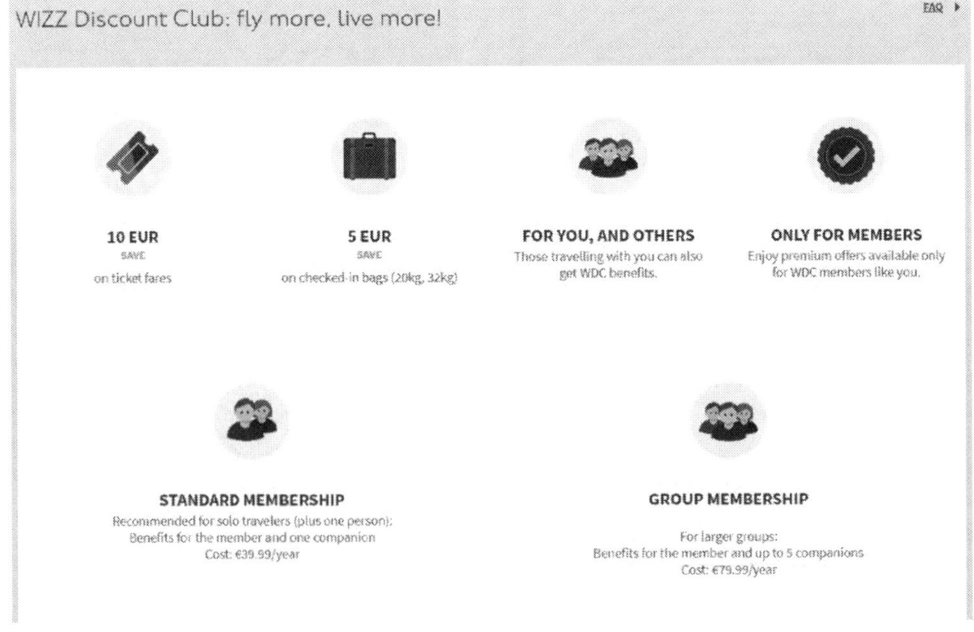

MEGAPOWERS	MEGAVOLOTEA	MEGAVOLOTEA PLUS
DISCOUNTS ON ALL YOUR FLIGHTS	Up to €10 discount per flight	Up to €15 discount per flight
DISCOUNTED LUGGAGE	Up to 15% discount	Up to 25% discount
DISCOUNTED SEATS	Up to 25% discount	Up to 50% discount
PRIORITY BOARDING	—	For all passengers
GIFTS ON YOUR BIRTHDAY	€20 of Volotea credit	€35 of Volotea credit
EXCLUSIVE AND EARLY OFFERS	Monthly	Monthly
ANNUAL USE OF YOUR BENEFITS	Unlimited	Unlimited
ACCOMPANYING BENEFICIARIES	Up to four people on your booking	Unlimited
FLIGHTS OR MEGAFLIGHTS?	€49.99/year	49.99€/year (+1 year's Megavolotea subscription)

In my opinion, these programs are most useful for two or more people traveling together, and the maximum amount of discount will be for 4 – 5 travelers.

Let's see how this discount works on an example of a typical WizzAir flight. Imagine that a married couple is flying from Vienna to Madrid and back (11/22 to 11/27) and also has baggage. They bought the membership of the Wizz Discount Club for €39.99. Now, let's compare the cost of the flight with and without the membership.

With the Wizz Discount Club membership, the flight will cost €14.99 + €17.49 = €32.48. Additionally, you will have to pay €28 for baggage. The total cost per person will be €60.48. Since two people are flying, we multiply the sum by two and get a flight cost of €120.96. They paid €39.99 for the Wizz Discount Club, and the total cost will be €160.97.

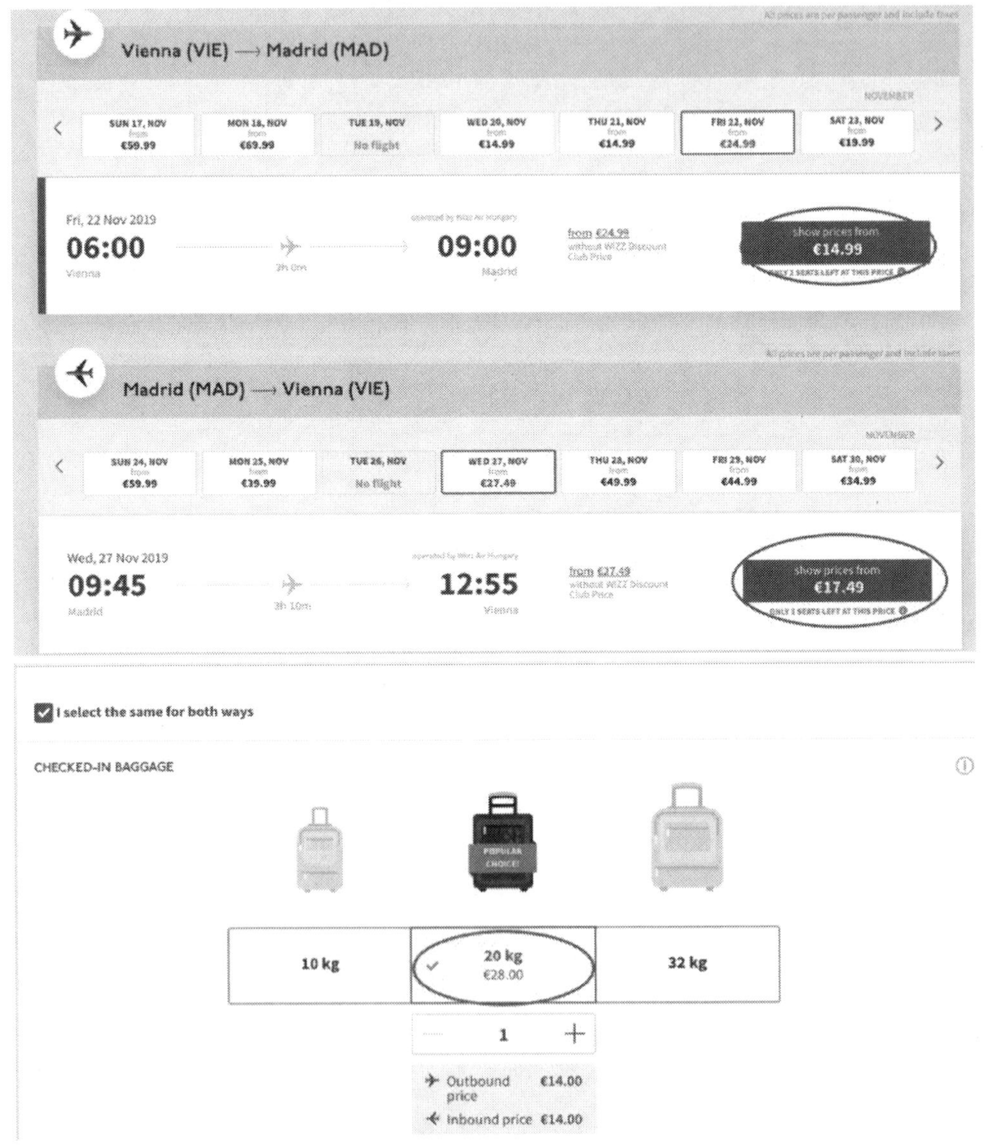

Without the Wizz Discount Club membership, the flight will cost €24.99 + €27.49 = €52.48. Additionally, you will have to pay €38 for baggage. The total cost per person will be €90.48, and for two, €180.96.

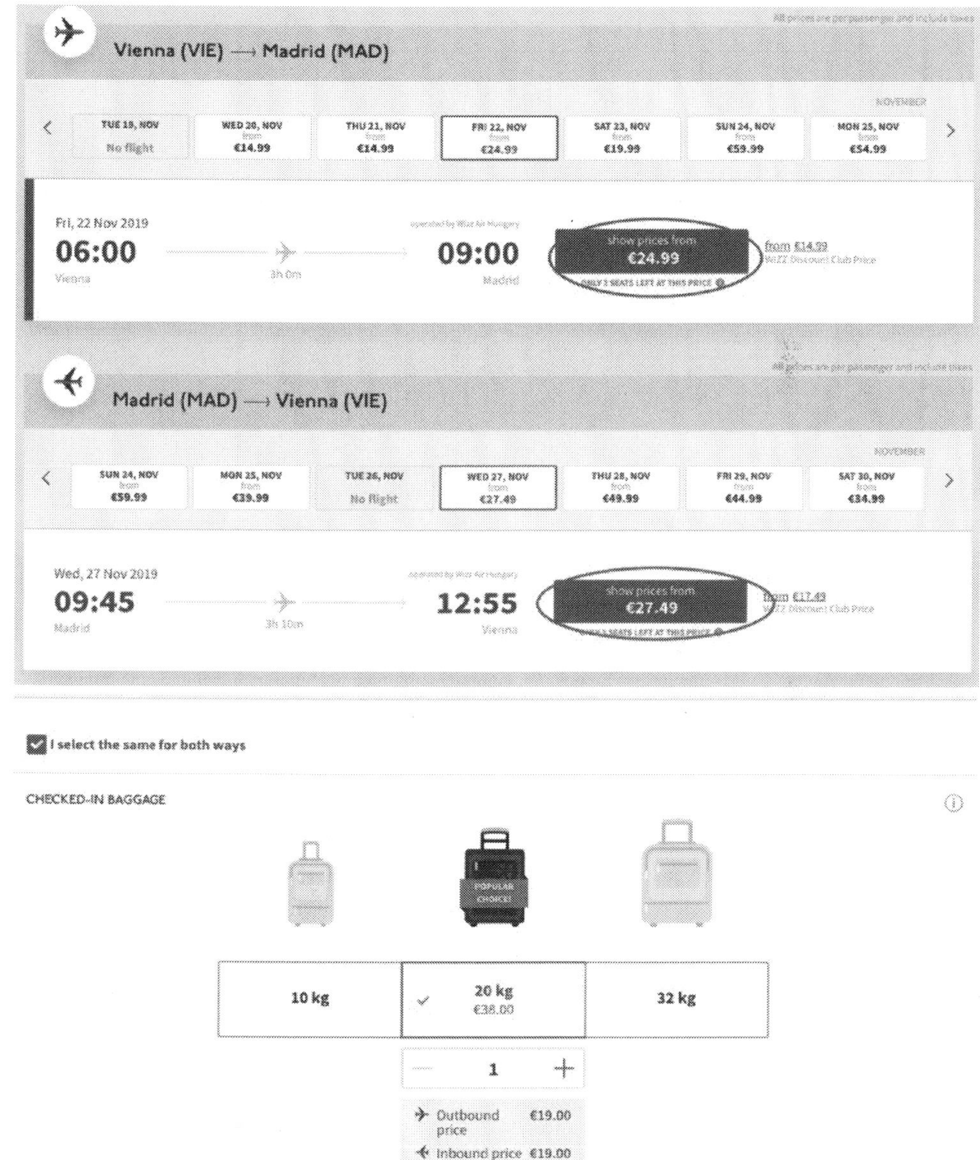

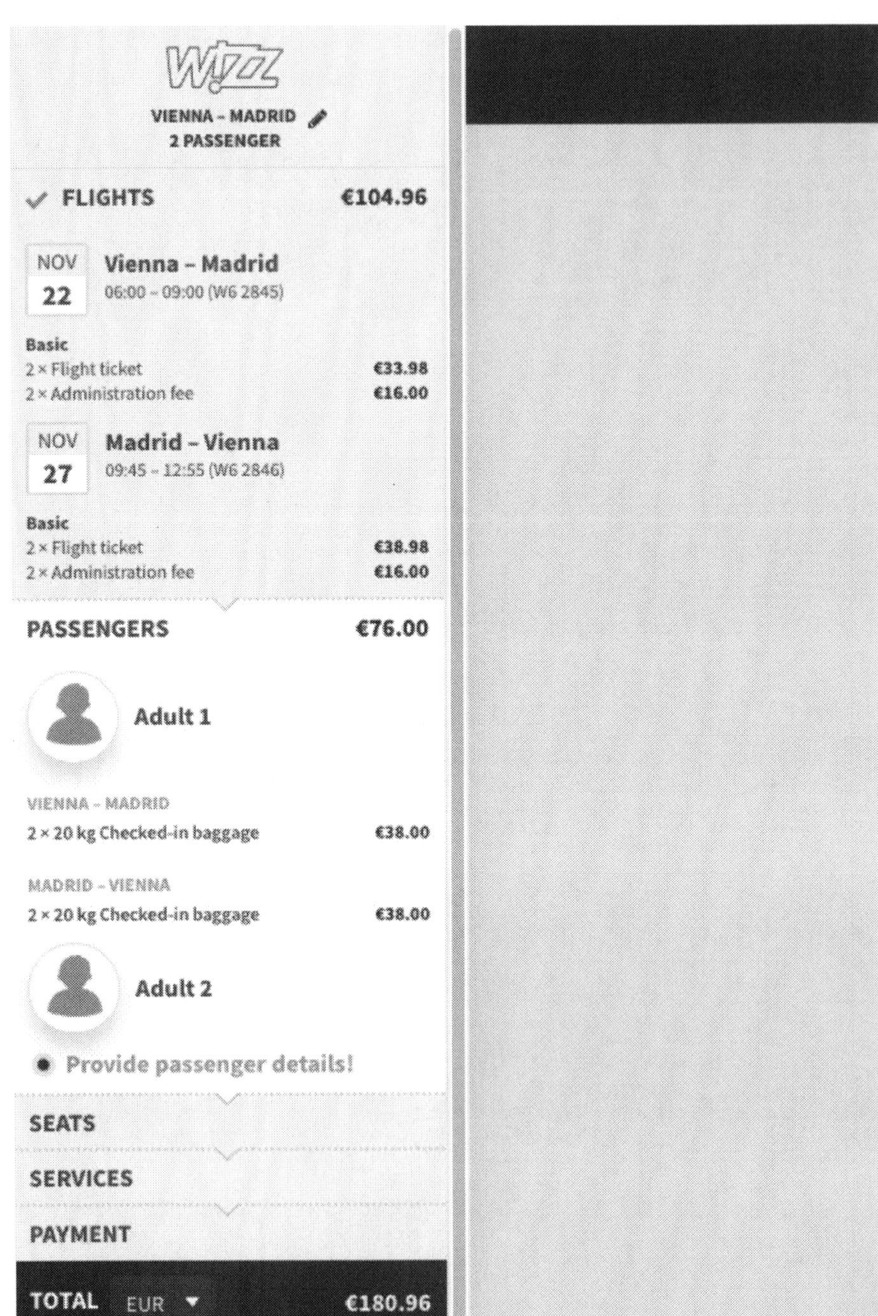
Wizz
VIENNA – MADRID
2 PASSENGER
FLIGHTS
€104.96
NOV
22
Vienna – Madrid
06:00 – 09:00 (W6 2845)
Basic
2 × Flight ticket
€33.98
2 × Administration fee
€16.00
NOV
27
Madrid – Vienna
09:45 – 12:55 (W6 2846)
Basic
2 × Flight ticket
€38.98
2 × Administration fee
€16.00
PASSENGERS
€76.00
Adult 1
VIENNA – MADRID
2 × 20 kg Checked-in baggage
€38.00
MADRID – VIENNA
2 × 20 kg Checked-in baggage
€38.00
Adult 2
Provide passenger details!
SEATS
SERVICES
PAYMENT
TOTAL
EUR
€180.96

When we compare the two amounts, you can see that the savings that you get for a round-trip flight are €19.99. And for all future trips with WizzAir, you will get even more significant savings, because you will no longer need to pay for the membership. And you'll get even more benefits if the membership is for six people, which costs €79.99.

After all, if we use the previous calculations, but count out the price for six people, we will see that with the Wizz Discount Club membership, the whole flight for six people would cost €60.48 × 6 + €79.99 = €442.93 and without the program: €90.48 × 6 = €542.88. That means the difference in price will be €100.

Buses/Trains

Quite often, while searching for the best travel route, you can find cheap bus tickets or ones that are on sale. Yes, of course, in most cases, it is less convenient than going by airplane — especially if you are traveling a long distance, and it would take 10, 20, or even 30 hours by bus.

Therefore, people choose to travel by bus when it is necessary to overcome short distances and when there are more bus routes in the needed direction than flights. You can also choose to go by bus only at night because you can significantly save on lodging. But traveling this way is undoubtedly tricky.

Buses can be especially convenient for those who cannot rent a car for some reason but, at the same time, want to see the nearest cities.

At the end of the book, you can find Appendix 2, which contains a list of the most popular bus companies.

Quite often, bus companies provide special offers, during which a small amount of the seats are being sold at a significant discount.

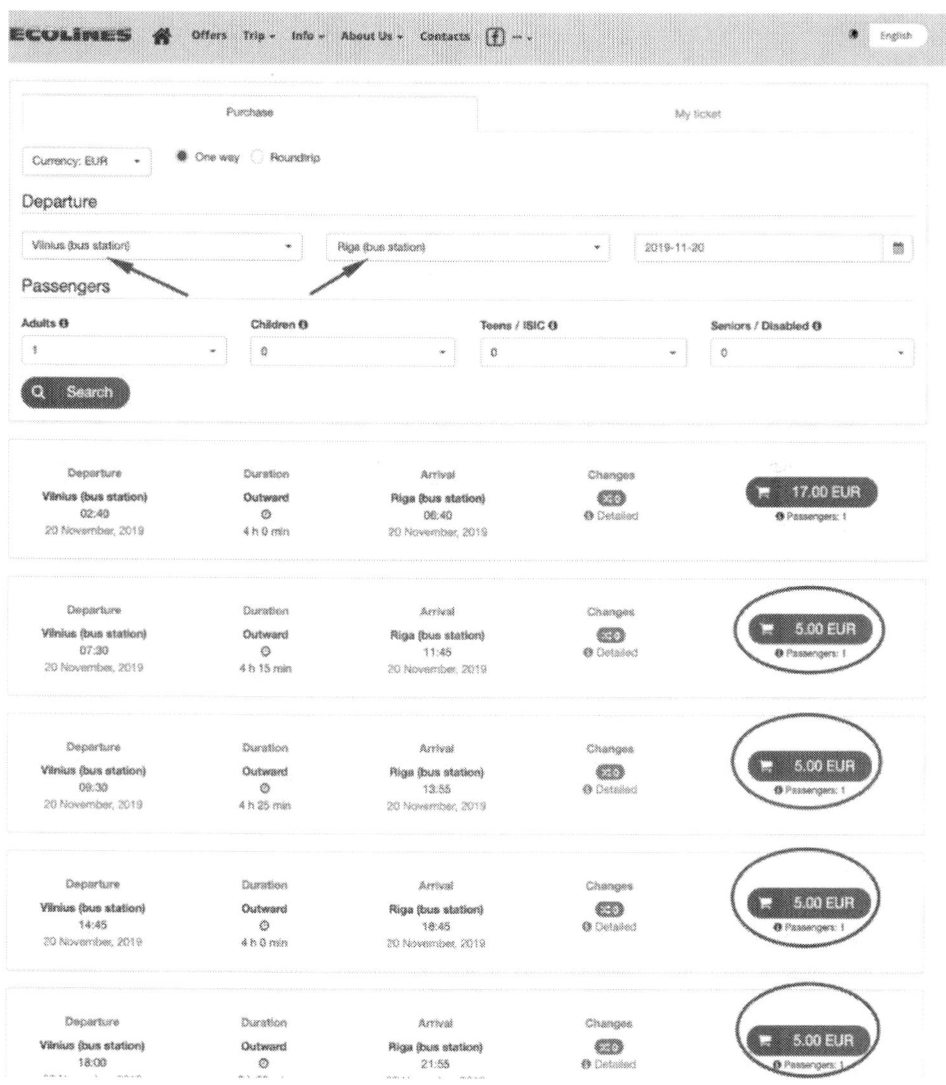
ECOLINES
Offers
Trip
Info
About Us
Contacts
English
Purchase
My ticket
Currency: EUR
One way
Roundtrip
Departure
Vilnius (bus station)
Riga (bus station)
2019-11-20
Passengers
Adults
Children
Teens / ISIC
Seniors / Disabled
Search
Departure
Vilnius (bus station)
02:40
20 November, 2019
Duration
Outward
4 h 0 min
Arrival
Riga (bus station)
06:40
20 November, 2019
Changes
Detailed
17.00 EUR
Passengers: 1
Vilnius (bus station)
07:30
20 November, 2019
4 h 15 min
Riga (bus station)
11:45
20 November, 2019
5.00 EUR
Passengers: 1
Vilnius (bus station)
09:30
20 November, 2019
4 h 25 min
Riga (bus station)
13:55
20 November, 2019
5.00 EUR
Vilnius (bus station)
14:45
20 November, 2019
4 h 0 min
Riga (bus station)
18:45
20 November, 2019
5.00 EUR
Vilnius (bus station)
18:00
Riga (bus station)
21:55
5.00 EUR

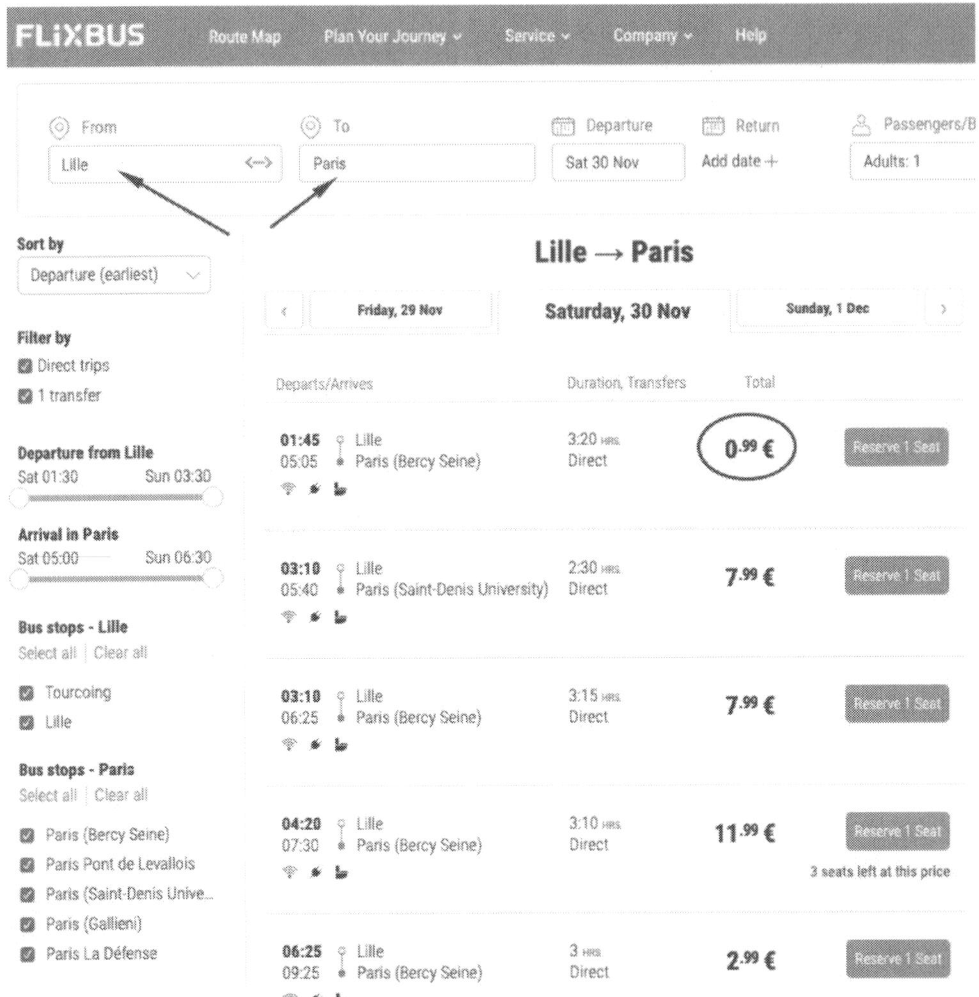

Trains are somewhat different from buses. Firstly, there are fewer affordable prices and discounts. In some countries (France, Switzerland), traveling by train is often more expensive than by plane. It is especially true for high-speed rails. But the train can also be used to build optimal travel routes.

We will look at specific examples of using tickets for buses and trains in the section below. Moreover, we will summarize the gained knowledge and create a complete travel route.

Cruises

What I'm about to tell you may sound strange, but cruises can sometimes be the best type of transport during a trip. After all, a cruise is not only a way to travel, but it is also a great opportunity to not pay for lodging. And, considering that almost all cruise companies pay a lot of attention to the entertainment programming onboard, you will not be bored.

I want to single out Scandinavia, the Baltic states, the Mediterranean Sea, and the Transatlantic as some great ones among the areas where you can save money on cruises.

The cheapest cruises are the ones in Scandinavia and the Baltic states. They are usually 1−2-day round-trip cruises. An excellent example of such one is the Oslo – Copenhagen – Oslo cruise, which costs €22 (NOK 220) per cabin (4 people). It means that each person pays €5.50 for a ride on a cruise liner from Oslo to Copenhagen and back, and a cabin for two nights. You will not find even a hostel for such a price in Copenhagen or Oslo.

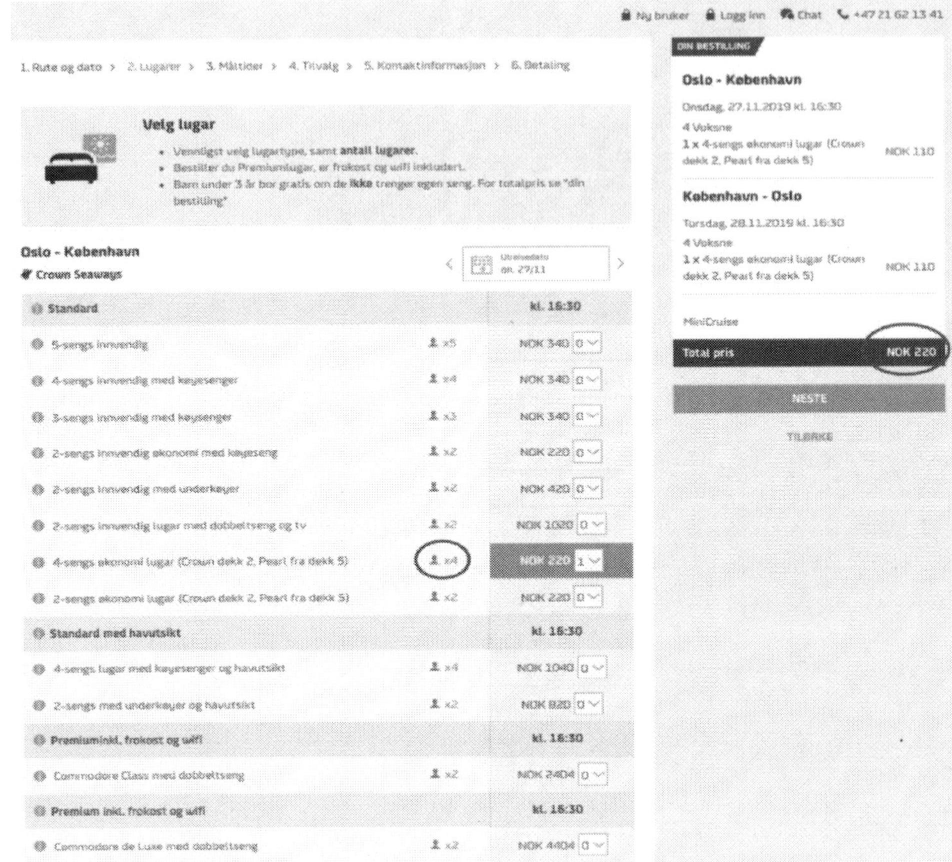

Mediterranean Sea cruises you can also use to get from one city to another. The prices there are usually higher, somewhere in the price range of €30 – 40 per person on the day. Also, fees may add to that price. Given the number of flights with low-cost airlines among European cities, this option will rarely be suitable for creating the best possible route.

Much more interesting are the options for transatlantic cruises. Firstly, tickets for flights from Europe and to the Caribbean/USA will be more expensive. Secondly, the cost of one day on a cruise ship is much lower — somewhere around $10 – 20. But you must keep in mind that the travel time of such a cruise usually takes at least seven days, if not more.

Itinéraire Bateau Vie à bord

27 Mars
2020
Changer de date

Intérieure
à partir de
€239

CONTINUER

:her la carte

16 jours (15 nuits) Transocéaniques au départ de Martinique

Bateau: Costa Favolosa Date : 27 Mars - 11 Avr. 2020
Départ: Martinique Arrivée: Marseille

Martinique, Guadeloupe, Îles Vierges britanniques, Espagne, Gibraltar, Italie, France

Lodging

Let's move on to the next section of the book, which is lodging — the second-most expensive part of traveling. In this section, you will find out what type of accommodation is better: an apartment or a room in a hotel.

Why Airbnb?

Airbnb is my favorite accommodation-searching platform. My opinion is, of course, subjective, but I will explain the reasons why I use it most often.

Firstly, the website contains discounts — weekly, monthly, during early booking, and even a one from the owner. You can contact the owner and ask them to give you a discount, but more about that a bit later.

Secondly, the platform has a vast number of apartment options. Surely, at least one of them will meet your needs.

Thirdly, unlike many other hotel booking services, this one makes it possible to book accommodations for more than 30 days.

And the most important part — I love living in my room — without housemaids, porters, reception, etc. Only then I can completely immerse myself in the life of locals — I visit their shops, eat at local restaurants, and walk wherever I want. And when I stay in a hotel, I always have the feeling that I am a guest and that everyone around is courting me, but at the same time, there is a feeling that this is not real, a game for which they are being paid money.

Airbnb Tricks

Well, let's move on to the ways that will allow you to prevent yourself from overpaying for lodging on Airbnb and even save money on it.

Trick 1. Self-cleaning

In my opinion, this is one of the not-so-awesome ways to save money on Airbnb. I have never tried it, but I will give you information about how to use it.

The point of this trick is to write to the owner before booking that you will clean the apartment by yourself after your stay.

This trick gives the following advantage — you get an opportunity to save money in cases where the cleaning fee is very high, like €30 and higher. It can be especially useful for short bookings, like for 1 – 2 days. Sometimes, it even happens that the cleaning fee is higher than both the accommodation and Airbnb fees summed up together.

But this method has some disadvantages. First, the owners not too often agree to this. Because they cannot be sure of the quality of your cleaning services. Secondly, for proper cleaning, you will need appropriate cleaning supplies, but usually, there are no such supplies in the apartment, since it's being rented, not lived in. And finally — a good cleaning is a long and challenging process. Are you ready for that?

Based on the information above, I would use this trick only when I get to stay in the apartment for one night with a high price for cleaning. Because after only one night, I wouldn't have so much cleaning to do so that the process will take little time and effort.

Trick 2. Ask for a discount for your review

This trick is much more interesting than the previous one, but I still wouldn't use it frequently. I have used it only a couple of times when traveling through cities with expensive lodging, and I asked the owners whether they could give me a small discount. And only once did I write what kind of discount I would like. In all other cases, I requested a "small discount."

I consider the fact that I didn't throw a pity party, didn't beg for the discount, and offered something essential and useful in return. When this worked, I wrote them positive and honest reviews from my account, which I have been using for a while and which has trust from both Airbnb and other users of that service.

The owners of brand-new housing or apartments on Airbnb and with a small number of reviews are most willing to give such discounts.

Trick 3. Book "NEW"

If you see the word "NEW" written in the housing description, it means that the owner has recently added it to the service.

Such apartments are usually cheaper. But there is a risk that the housing will turn out to not as you expected because there are almost no reviews for such apartments, and you can't verify the quality.

On the other hand, "NEW" owners are often more accommodating than rated homeowners because they need good reviews to appear higher on Airbnb searches.

Brussels · Stays

2 guests | Work trip | Entire place | Up to $40 | Instant Book | More filters

3 places to stay

ENTIRE APARTMENT

Lighthouse apartment

2 guests · 1 bedroom · 1 bed · 1 bath

Wifi · Kitchen · Free parking · Heating

$28/night
$32 total

ENTIRE LOFT

Kunstzinnige loft

RARE FIND · This place is usually booked.

2 guests · 1 bedroom · 1 bed · 1 bath

Wifi · Kitchen · Heating

★4.82 (240) · Superhost

$39/night
$44 total

ENTIRE HOUSE

simplicity is the key to the elegance..

RARE FIND · This place is usually booked.

2 guests · Studio · 1 bed · 1 bath

Wifi · Kitchen · Heating

★3.71 (45)

$38/night
$62 total

Trick 4. Long-term lease

If you book an apartment through Airbnb service for one week, or longer, you can get a discount. The owner determines its size. The most attractive offers are possible when renting apartments for one month or more.

Here is an example of booking apartments in Brussels (Belgium) for two days, 14 days, and 28 days. If you book it for two days, the price is $175, and for 14 days, there is already a small discount, and the total amount is $854. For 28 days, there is a perfect discount — $986 for the entire period. As can be seen from the numbers, the difference between 28 and 14 days: $986 – $854 = $132.

And if you take this number and divide it by the difference in the number of days (14), we can see that each day will cost $9.43. For Brussels, this is an unrealistically low price.

In my practice, there were such funny situations when paying for an apartment for a month was the same or even cheaper than renting it for two weeks. So booking a room on Airbnb for an extended period is an excellent way to save money.

Appartement typique bruxellois RDC

Vorst

- **Entire apartment**
  2 guests 2 bedrooms 2 beds 1 bath
- **Amenities for everyday living**
  The host has equipped this place for long stays - kitchen, wifi, washer, and heating included.
- **Guests love this place for long stays**
  100% of guests who've stayed a month or longer have reviewed this place as 5 stars.
- **Sparkling clean**
  10 recent guests said this place was sparkling clean.

Translate this description to English

Rez de chaussée de style typiquement bruxellois à une minute du grand parc de

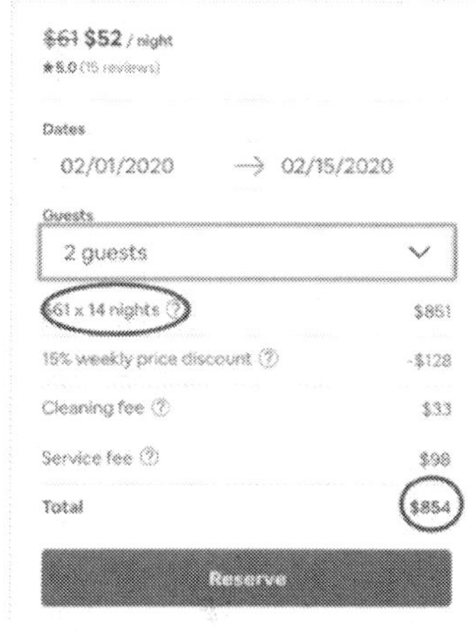

Appartement typique bruxellois RDC

Vorst

- **Entire apartment**
  2 guests 2 bedrooms 2 beds 1 bath
- **Amenities for everyday living**
  The host has equipped this place for long stays - kitchen, wifi, washer, and heating included.
- **Guests love this place for long stays**
  100% of guests who've stayed a month or longer have reviewed this place as 5 stars.
- **Sparkling clean**
  10 recent guests said this place was sparkling clean.

Translate this description to English

Rez de chaussée de style typiquement bruxellois à une minute du grand parc de

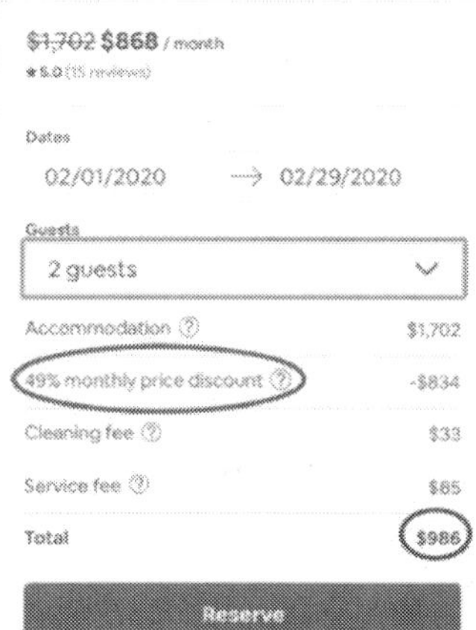

Trick 5. Book an apartment in the off-season long before the trip

Prices of most apartments on Airbnb depend on whether it is peak season or off-season. It means that in one period, prices will be significantly lower than in another. For example, the cities of the Mediterranean coast have a trend of expensive summers and cheaper winters. Or Alsace (France), where prices are significantly higher during Christmas.

Many apartment-owners set the prices themselves and do not have a complicated calendar with prices for every season. For example, if apartment prices in winter are lower, there is a good chance of booking a house in the winter for the summer, you will receive a confirmation from the owner to rent an apartment for the summer at winter prices.

So, it can be better to rent an apartment beforehand when it costs lower than to rent it at a higher price at the peak season when competition between owners on Airbnb will also increase.

I will give some examples of bookings using this method.

If you book an apartment in Heraklion (Crete, Greece) now, it will cost $300 for the whole month of August. Typically, in the summer, housing there will cost at least $40 per day. But if you book it now, it will cost $10 per day.

Studio 2.7 Budget studio near city center

Iraklio

Entire apartment
2 guests Studio 1 bed 1 bath

Amenities for everyday living
The host has equipped this place for long stays - kitchen, wifi, washer, and dryer included.

Guests love this place for long stays
100% of guests who've stayed a month or longer have reviewed this place as 5 stars.

Self check-in
Check yourself in with the lockbox.

Budget studio in Therissos Heraklion, Crete. 5 minutes walking from Bus Station to various locations in Crete. 10 minutes walking from city center. Near places of interest, convenient stores, eateries. Quiet, safe, local neighborhood. Special Deals for Erasmus students for long stays! It has window on the street, no balcony. We pick your laundry. 2.5 euros per washing, 2 euros for dryer. We only do communication through AIRBNB messaging. We do not reply by SMS or call to International numbers

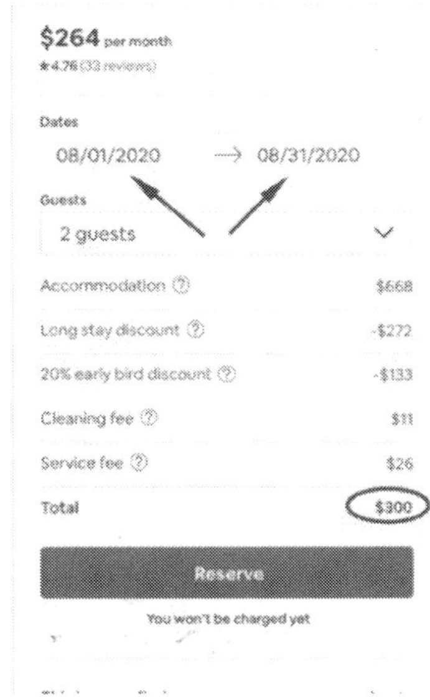

An apartment in Sicily (Italy) will cost $415 for the whole of July. The usual price in July is $45 per day and above.

Nei luoghi di Montalbano - La Sicilia che volevi!

Antonio

Donnalucata

Entire house
5 guests 2 bedrooms 4 beds 1 bath

Amenities for everyday living
The host has equipped this place for long stays - kitchen, washer, pets allowed, and ac included.

Translate this description to English

A pochi metri dalla spiaggia di Donnalucata.
Casa indipendente. Pianterreno.
Composta da, un salottino con TV all'ingresso,una luminosa camera matrimoniale, una cameretta con tre letti singoli sfruttabile anche come seconda matrimoniale, un bagno finestrato con box doccia e lavatrice, cucina abitabile, una spaziosa veranda.

Per chi non conosce la zona, forniamo volentieri indicazioni varie sulle migliori

~~$597~~ $346 / month
★4.60 (5 reviews)

Dates
07/01/2020 → 07/31/2020

Guests
2 guests

Accommodation	$597
42% monthly price discount	-$251
Cleaning fee	$33
Service fee	$36
Total	$415

Reserve

A house in Sardinia (Italy) will cost $356 for the period from July 1 to July 31; whereas, the standard price in the summer is $50 per day and above.

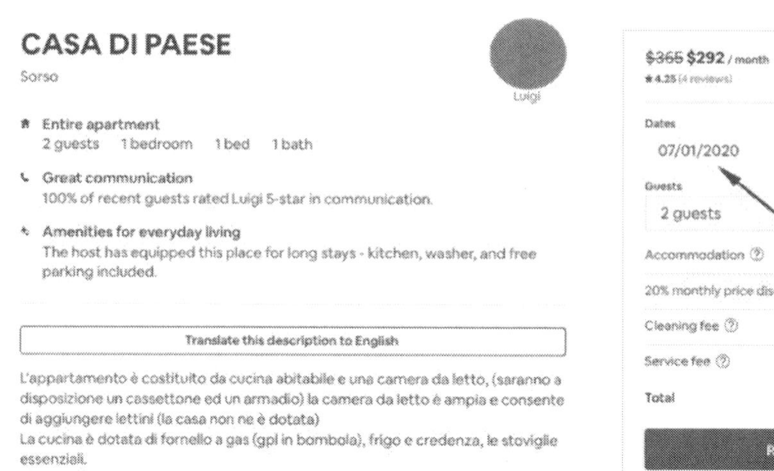

A studio in Cannes (France) will cost $696 in July. Cannes is a costly and prestigious resort. During summer, they can ask $70 and above per day for a studio.

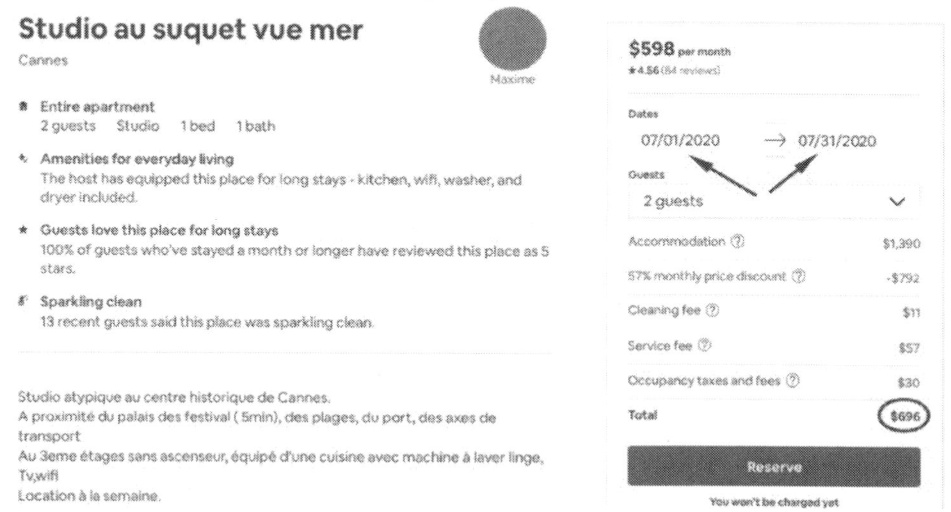

An apartment for six people in Alicante (Spain) will cost $560 per month. So, it will cost $93 per person per month. In July, the usual price for such a house with a good rating and costs around $100 per day for six people.

Charming apartment in Alicante

Alacant

Ionut

★ **Entire apartment**
6 guests 2 bedrooms 5 beds 1 bath

Amenities for everyday living
The host has equipped this place for long stays - kitchen, wifi, ac, and heating included.

★ **Guests love this place for long stays**
100% of guests who've stayed a month or longer have reviewed this place as 5 stars.

Sparkling clean
3 recent guests said this place was sparkling clean.

Charming apartment, recently renovated! Located in a popular and authentic area, very close to all amenities, less than 100 meters walk transport (tram and bus), supermarkets, pharmacy, tobacco, hairdresser .... I will be very happy to welcome and advise you on your trip to Alicante!

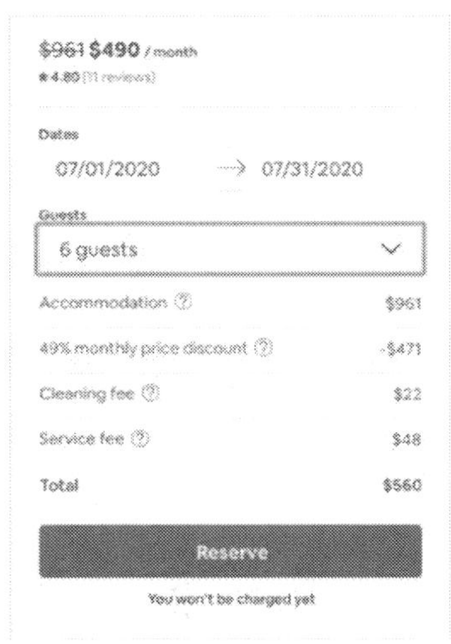

The only disadvantage of this method is that you should be ready to book accommodations 3 – 6 months before the trip.

Trick 6. Rent housing somewhere nearby, but with the ability to quickly and conveniently get to the right place

This method is suitable for you if you plan to visit cities with expensive rents during your trip. Such cities include Amsterdam, Paris, or Barcelona. It will cost you at least $70 – 80 to rent an apartment in such towns. And then the amount of choices is small. But if you take housing in the suburbs, with the ability to get to the desired city quickly and for a small fee, you can find an option 2 – 3 times cheaper.

For example, if you wish to go on a Christmas vacation to Amsterdam, the minimum price for an apartment in the city center will be $143 per day. And in the suburbs, it will be $111.

2 places to stay

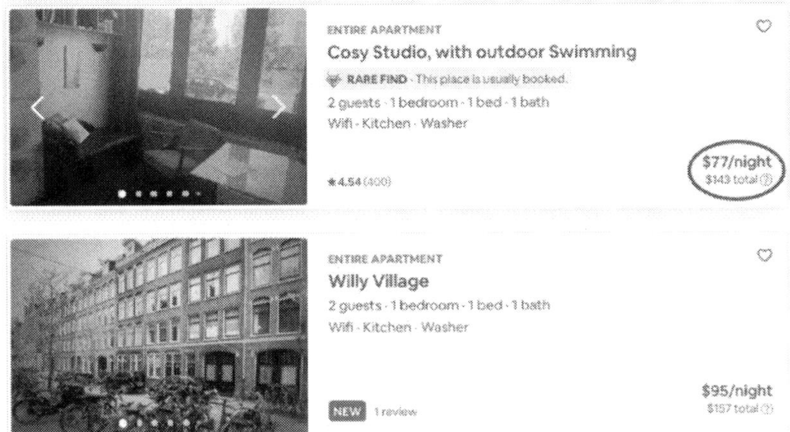

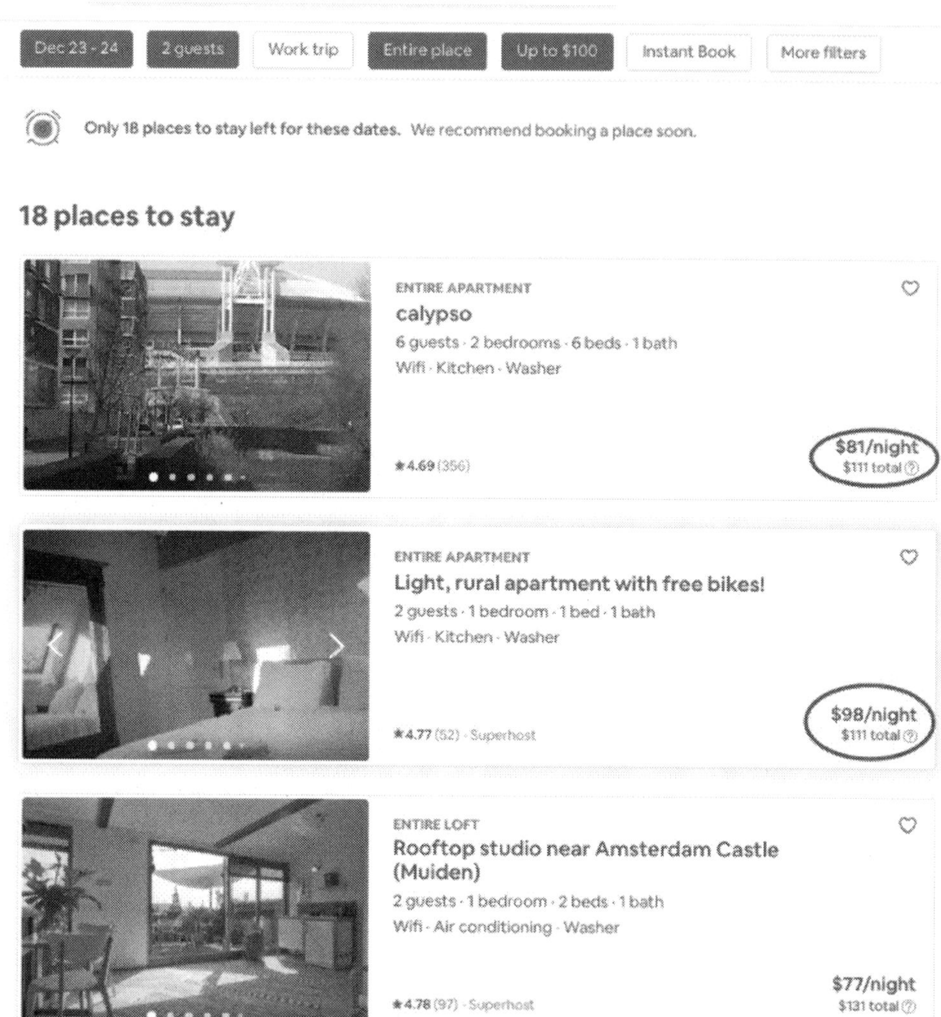

Now let's consider the nearest cities that are about an hour's drive from Amsterdam. From the several options that we have, the most suitable one, in my opinion, was apartments in Wormer ($61 per day). They have outstanding ratings.

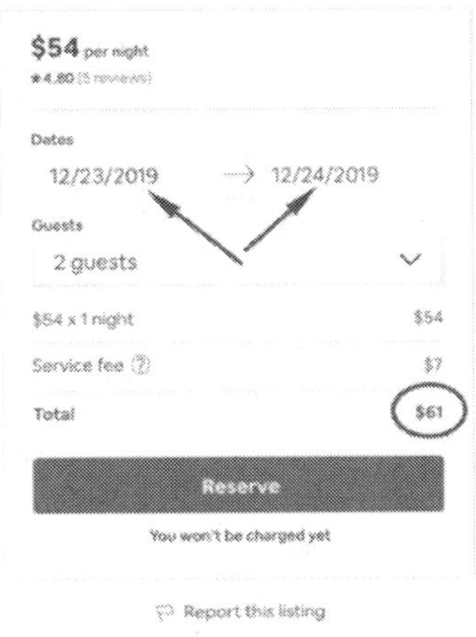

Moreover, the apartment description says that there is a train nearby that can take you to the center of Amsterdam in 20 minutes. I looked up the information on the official website, and it is true — the travel time is 21 minutes, and it costs €3.90, which is slightly more than $4. Or you can also buy a ticket for a round trip, which will cost $8.50 for one person. If you are buying it for two people, it will cost $17.

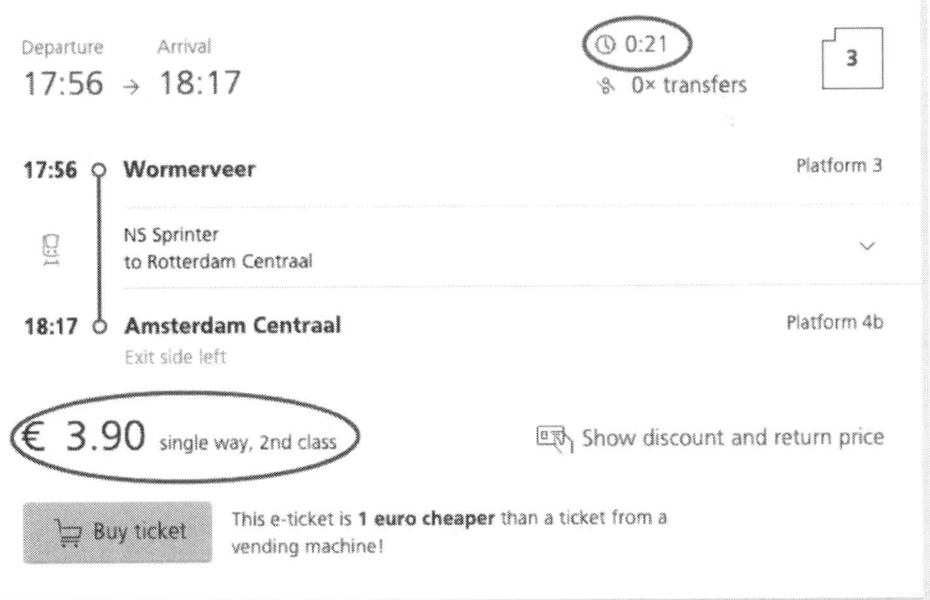

If you compare the price for an apartment in the suburbs of Amsterdam with the one in the nearby cities, you will see that there is a difference in $50. But remember, the disadvantage of renting an apartment in neighboring cities is that you will spend time and money to get to the center. But if you compare the apartment price to the one in the city center, you will save even more — $82. So, whether the difference in price is $50, or $86, it is more than $17. And 20 minutes is a little time, so you won't regret that you spent it on a train.

But this trick does have some disadvantages. The larger the group of people, the lower the savings. Everyone will need to pay for round-trip transportation.

Trick 7. Search for apartments without typing in the dates

This way is the most engaging, in my opinion, but at the same time, it is quite a long one. Usually, a person who is looking for an apartment on Airbnb enters the dates they need and looks at all options and finds the one that suits them best. But Airbnb offers the ability to search for apartments without typing in the desired dates.

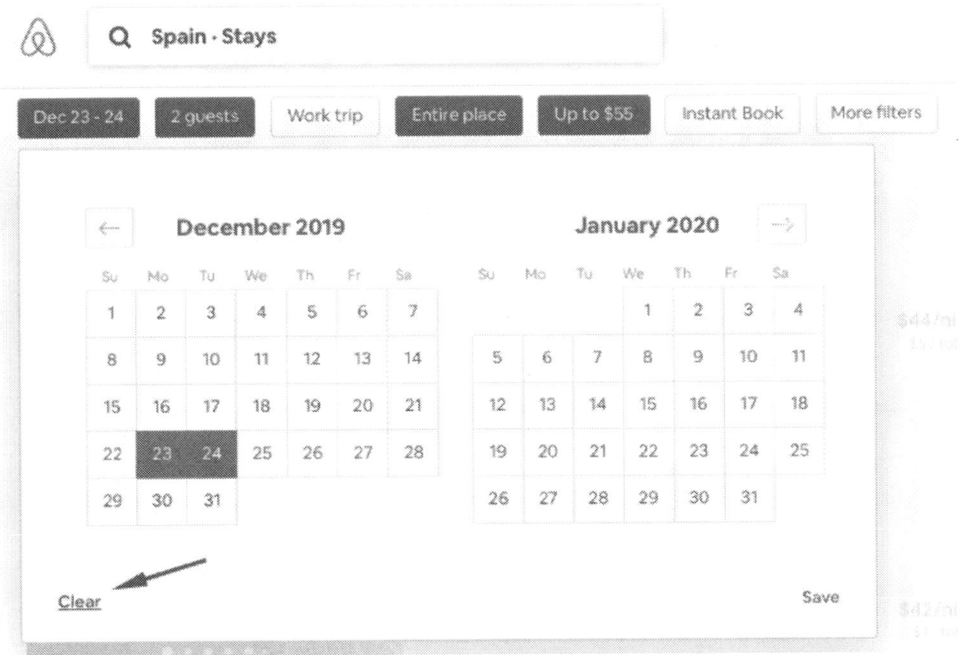

If you don't enter any dates, you only need to select the city in which you want to find an apartment, and you'll get all possible housing options with the lowest prices. Then, you can filter the received results by the desired price, by setting the maximum price that you are willing to pay per day and consider all options with such a price and lower.

Open the descriptions of all the apartments you like and see how much they intersect with the dates you need and how much they will cost on the selected dates. In the end, you usually get, instead of one option for the entire duration of the trip, several that intersect.

Such a method has the main disadvantage — you will need to move from one apartment to another within the same city. Well, the big plus is that the price of several flats will be lower than for one for the entire period of your stay.

Let's look at an example. We want to stay in Prague for November 18 – 23. A regular search gives us the cheapest option at $184. So it will cost $184 ÷ 5 = $37 per day.

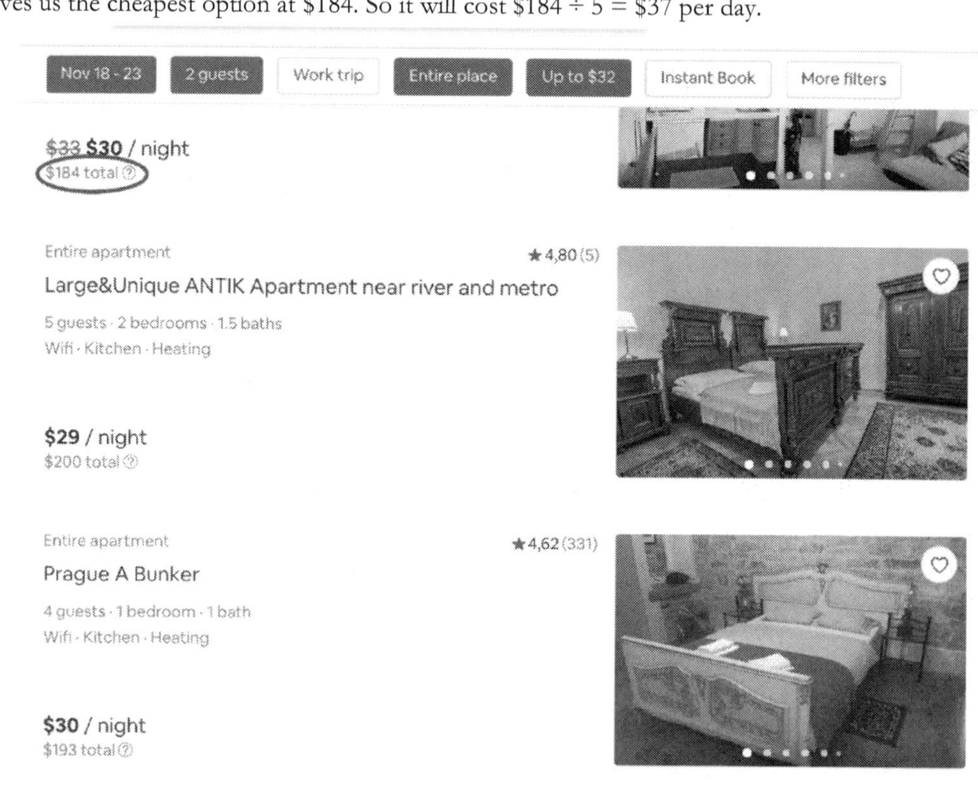

After that, let's clear the date search box and set the highest price that might interest us. If, in the previous search, it turned out that we will need to pay at least $37 per day, then let's set the maximum price of $25.

Prague · Stays

Dates | 2 guests | Work trip | Entire place | Up to $25 | Instant Book | More filters

Over 660,000 guest reviews for places to stay in Prague, with an average of 4.7 out of 5 stars.

96 places to stay

SUPERHOST Entire apartment ★4,76 (274)

Romantic and Quiet Apartment, 15 min from center

2 guests · Studio · 1 bath
Wifi · Kitchen · Heating

$13 / night

Entire apartment ★4,77 (252)

Terrace Apartment with private bathroom

2 guests · 1 bedroom · 1.5 baths
Wifi · Heating

$24 / night

We received 96 housing options with a price of $25 per day and lower. But it may turn out that, on the needed dates, the apartment is occupied, or the price for it will be above $25 because now we see the lowest prices, but not the price for the desired dates. And now, we need to check whether the apartments that we like are available so that we could rent them on the desired dates.

Logically, there won't be only one apartment available with a price of $25 and lower for the entire period of November 18 – 23, because otherwise, we would have seen it on the first search with a price lower than $184 for the whole period. Therefore, there will most likely be two apartments that will be available on different days from November 18 to 23.

And having done such a search, I found these two apartments. The first needs to be booked for November 18 – 21, which costs $92, and the second for November 21 – 23, which costs

$61. And the total price for those two apartments is $153, which is $31 lower than what we got from the initial search.

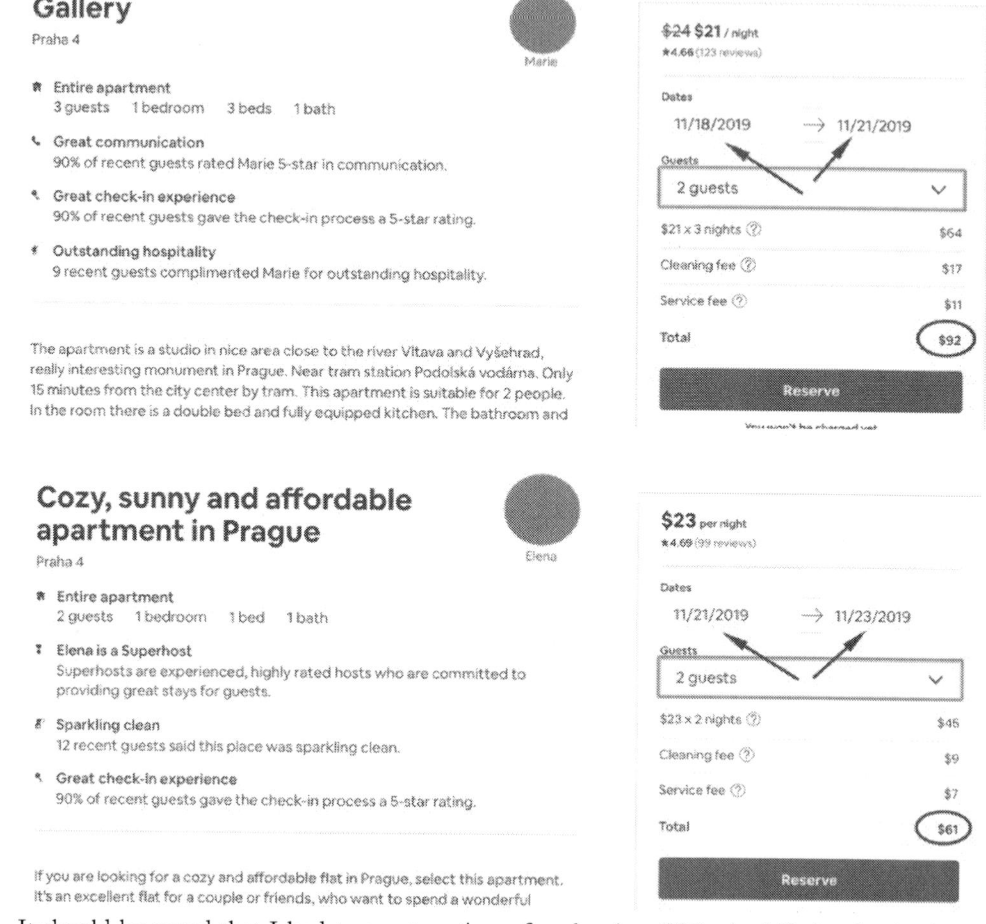

It should be noted that I had to pay two times for cleaning ($26). And if cleaning in these two apartments is expensive, then booking two separate ones instead of one will not be so profitable.

Hotel Booking

I am not a fan of staying at a hotel. I wrote about the reasons for my point of view earlier. But still, many people do prefer hotels over apartments. Moreover, hotels have some advantages on Airbnb — the possibility of free cancellation, because on the Airbnb website, in case of a cancellation, a small part of the payment will not be returned.

A good option is to use Booking or Agoda as backup services. Well, imagine that you are not able to find a suitable apartment on the Airbnb platform and decide on a room on Booking with a free cancelation option, and if after some time, you do find a suitable variant on Airbnb, you can easily cancel the previous booking.

It is also worth noting that Airbnb is not very popular in some countries, and it may turn out that Booking or Agoda has many more options, including apartments. As an example, some such countries are Asia, Albania, and Montenegro.

Now let's move on to the ways that can help you save on hotels.

Trick 1. Call the hotel directly

It is a straightforward solution. First, select a suitable hotel on Booking, and then find the hotel's phone number. After that, call the owner directly and try to negotiate a lower price. This trick usually works well with small hotels.

Here are some of the ins and outs regarding this trick: it is better to call the owner and communicate with them in their language. Do not use email, as the owners of such hotels rarely check it.

Trick 2. Book a hotel a few days before the trip

If there are a lot of rooms left in a hotel, they are often ready to provide a good discount, because otherwise, no one will book rooms, and they will not earn anything at all.

Many services provide such offerings, such as Priceline or Hotwire. An interesting feature of these services is that you do not see the name of the hotel before booking. The owners themselves insist on this, because if everyone sees that the hotel is giving out such a big discount, then when booking it without a discount, people will consider it to be expensive.

Since you will be taking a big risk when waiting until the last days before the trip, you may end up without a suitable offer at all. That is why it is better to have a backup option. For example, you can book a room on the Booking website with the possibility of cancellation a day before the check-in.

Trick 3. Discounts, cashback, special offers

You can often find various limited-time special offers and discounts on hotel booking websites, such as "invite a friend and get a refund from their first trip," "get a 10% discount on booking," etc.

But in fact, these are all marketing tricks. These discounts are usually of short duration, and conditions can be interpreted in favor of the service (in fact, I've often heard that payments were canceled due to a fictitious violation of the rules).

The only exception is the Genius Booking program, which has been running for a very long time and gives a small discount for some hotels. To get Genius status, you need to make a certain number of trips: for level 1, it takes two travels in 2 years, for level 2, it's five trips in 2 years.

How to plan the best possible trip

In this section, I will tell you how to use the knowledge you gained earlier and plan the perfect trip.

Any trip usually starts in one place and ends at another one. In most cases, this is the same city, generally being the place where you typically live or a place nearby. These two places will be our location A and location B. We will use them to plan the trip.

We can begin to plan our trip with location A and look for options near it, or we can begin with location B. I will provide you with an example for a better understanding. Imagine that you want to go somewhere for a month, from July 1 – August 1. And you live in New York. In this case, we have two options with which we can begin building the route.

The first option is to decide which country you want to visit (if you have already chosen it, then we are looking for the most optimal way to get there). The second option is to look from which country it is best to fly back to New York on August 1 (if we know where we will be at the end of the trip, then we need to find the cheapest way to get to New York from there).

I often use the first option because it's easier to go from beginning to end than vice versa. But sometimes I come across perfect offers for the return flight, for example, a flight from Madrid to New York that costs $40 – 50. And in such cases, I start building the route from the end of the trip.

Now imagine that you have created one route, then the second. And you want to compare it with each other and determine which one you like best. Each itinerary consists of flights, bus trips, and apartments. It is pretty complicated and inconvenient to write it all down somewhere on paper or in a notebook. That's why it is necessary to keep all that information in an electronic format so that it is convenient to look through all the data from a laptop or smartphone.

I tried out many apps, but none had the functionality that I wanted. And then, I concluded that it is most convenient to collect data on travel routes in the usual Google Sheets. If you are familiar with applications or websites that allow you to perform what I will show below, then please write about it in the reviews of my book, and I will definitely check them out and add them to this book, as well as mention you in the thank you section.

Here is how my Google Sheets template looks:

A	B	C	D	E	F	G
Start Date	End Date	Expense Item	Where From	Where To	Cost	Days

April 2020

In the table, you can keep records of such data: start and end dates of the travel segment, expense item (the sum of money that will be spent on lodging, flight tickets, bus tickets, etc.), where the travel segment starts at and where it ends, cost, and number of days in this segment.

Next, I will show you how to fill out this template. You can use it as an example, or make any changes to it that you consider necessary.

Imagine that a married couple wants to visit Italy in February 2020. They live in London. It will be their first time in Italy. The purpose of planning is to select several interesting routes and compare them with each other. Since it is better to use one currency for comparison and budget management, I will use the euro.

To start, I will look at all the possible flights from London to Italy in February.

It turns out that there are a lot of options that cost €20 and below for one-way travel. I took into account that this is the winter season, so beaches will not be a part of this trip. Since our couple has never been to Italy before, I will focus on the most popular cities. Also, the Carnival in Venice, which will be held on February 8 – 25, is an event that is worth seeing during this period. The most exciting part of the Carnival is the beginning or the end one. So Venice will be either at the start or the end of the route. Among other famous cities are Rome, Florence,

Milan, Naples, Pisa. I would choose four places so that there will be enough time to explore them fully. So, I want Venice, Rome, Florence, and some other city.

First, let's create a route with Venice as the starting point. That's why we should look for available flights from London to Venice in early February. It turns out that the best way is to fly on February 1 for €18. For two it will cost €36. Type this information into Google Sheets.

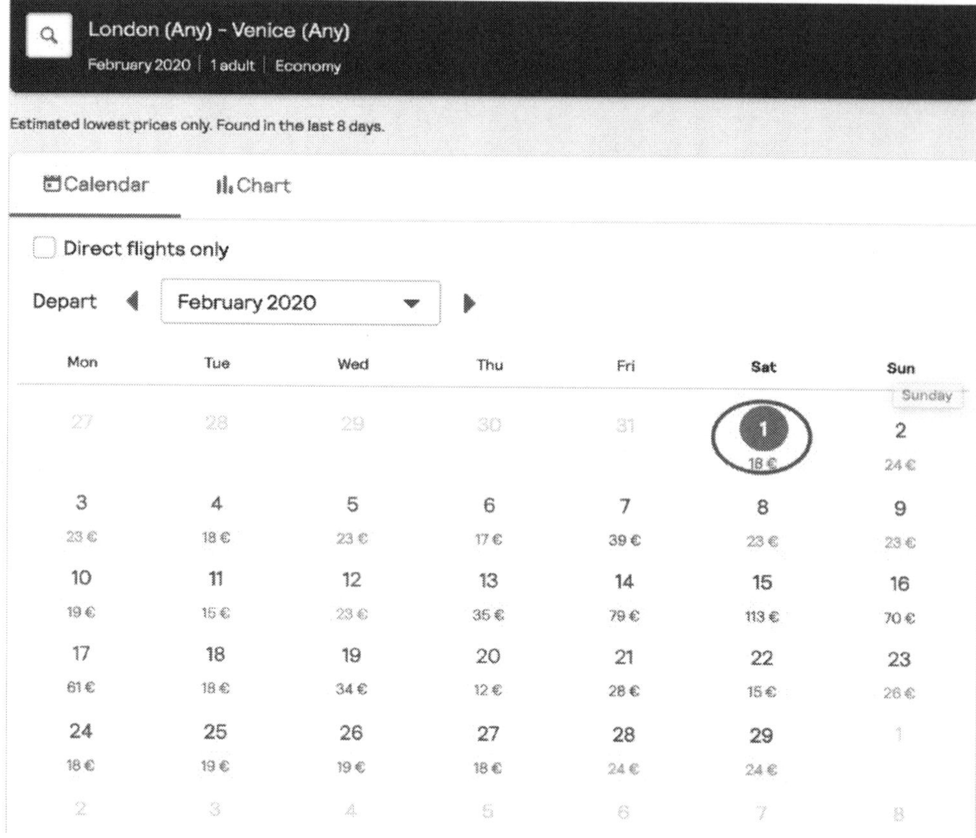

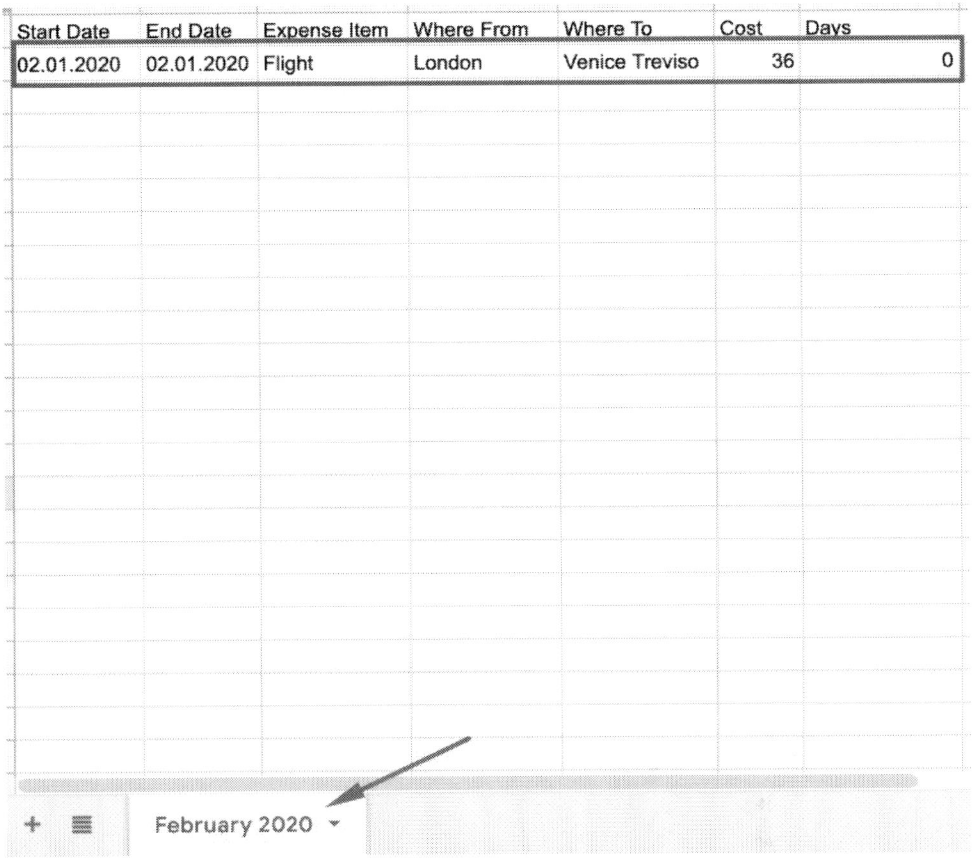

Start Date	End Date	Expense Item	Where From	Where To	Cost	Days
02.01.2020	02.01.2020	Flight	London	Venice Treviso	36	0

\+ ≣ February 2020 ▾

The next step is to find accommodation in Venice. First, let's look at Airbnb and then on Booking. Since our couple wants to attend the opening of the Carnival, we select the following dates: February 1 – 9.

The best option in the center of Venice costs €430 for this period. It is an apartment with a kitchen, Wi-Fi and has a 4.33 rating, out of a possible 5.

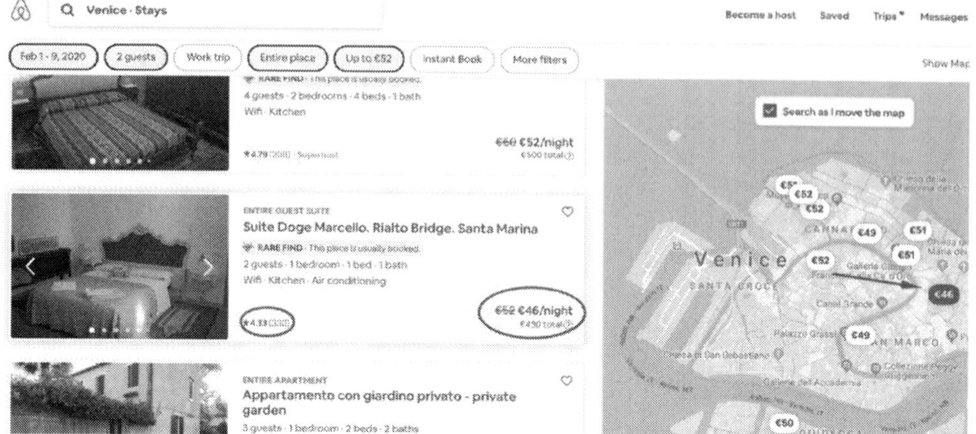

From the information that I provided earlier, we remember that you need to look for lodging options in the nearby cities. The most interesting option is Mestre. This city has a light rail. In Mestre, you can use the light rail to get to Venice. It costs €1.35, and the travel time is 10 – 15 minutes.

Partenza		Arrivo	Durata	Treno	Prezzo
Venezia Mestre 20:06	→	Venezia S. Lucia 20:16	0h 10'	Regionale 33777	da 1,35 €
Venezia Mestre 20:10	→	Venezia S. Lucia 20:20	0h 10'	Regionale Veloce 2218	da 1,35 €
Venezia Mestre 20:18	→	Venezia S. Lucia 20:30	0h 12'	Regionale Veloce 2244	da 1,35 €
Venezia Mestre 20:24	→	Venezia S. Lucia 20:34	0h 10'	Regionale 5781	da 1,35 €
Venezia Mestre 20:34	→	Venezia S. Lucia 20:46	0h 12'	Regionale 11077	da 1,35 €

Keep in mind that lodging in Mestre is much cheaper. For the period from February 1 to February 9, there are options for €252 (NEW, without Wi-Fi, poor transport accessibility — far from the light rail), €303 (rating 4.82, has a kitchen, Wi-Fi, near the light rail stop). You can certainly take the cheaper option, but in my opinion, it is not worth it. Therefore, I choose the second one.

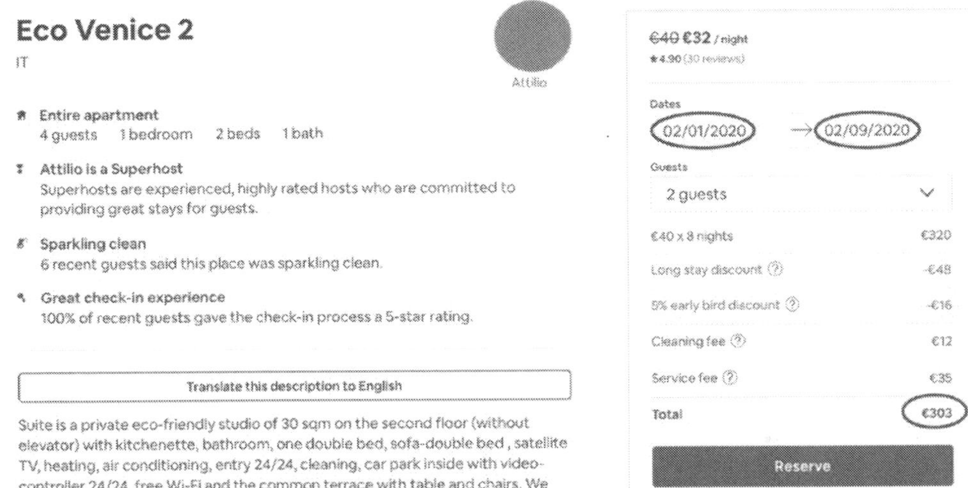

Next, let's see what options does Booking.com give us. The cheapest option in the center of Venice is €438 plus €82 of taxes. In Mestre: €310 + €89. Both options are more expensive than similar ones on Airbnb, so they are not taken into account in the creation of the route.

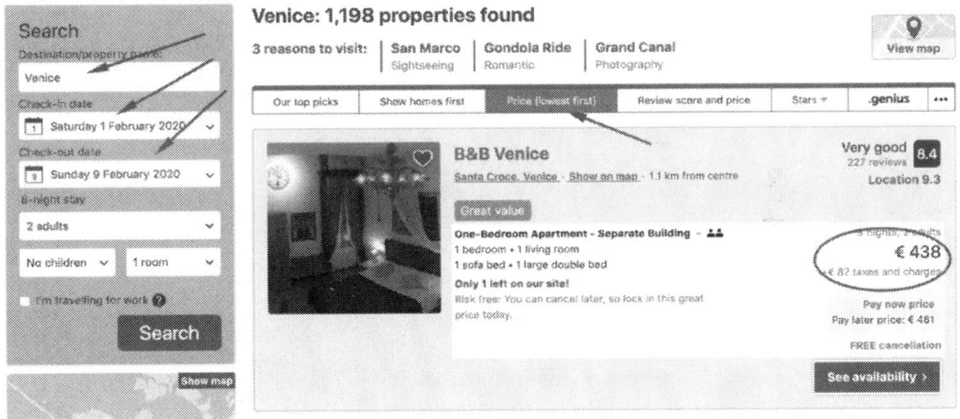

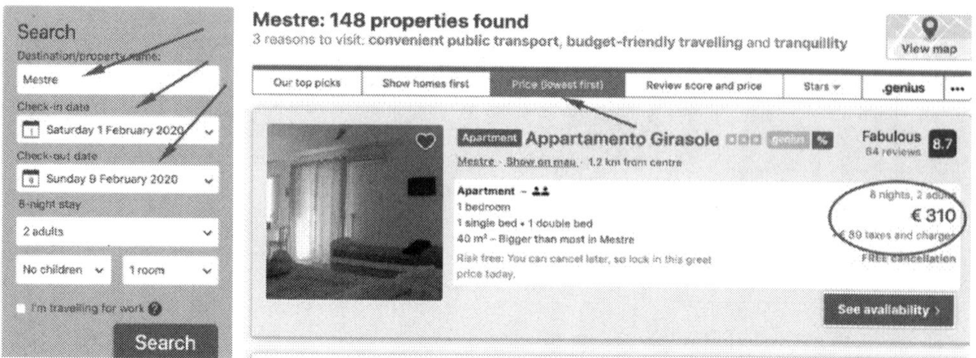

Now that we have chosen an arrival airport and a lodging place, we need to find a way to get from the airport to the apartment. We will use the Rome2Rio service (for a detailed description of the service, see Appendix 3). Go to the website and choose Venice Treviso Airport (TSF) and Mestre, and you will get different options. The most suitable one was the Trenitalia train.

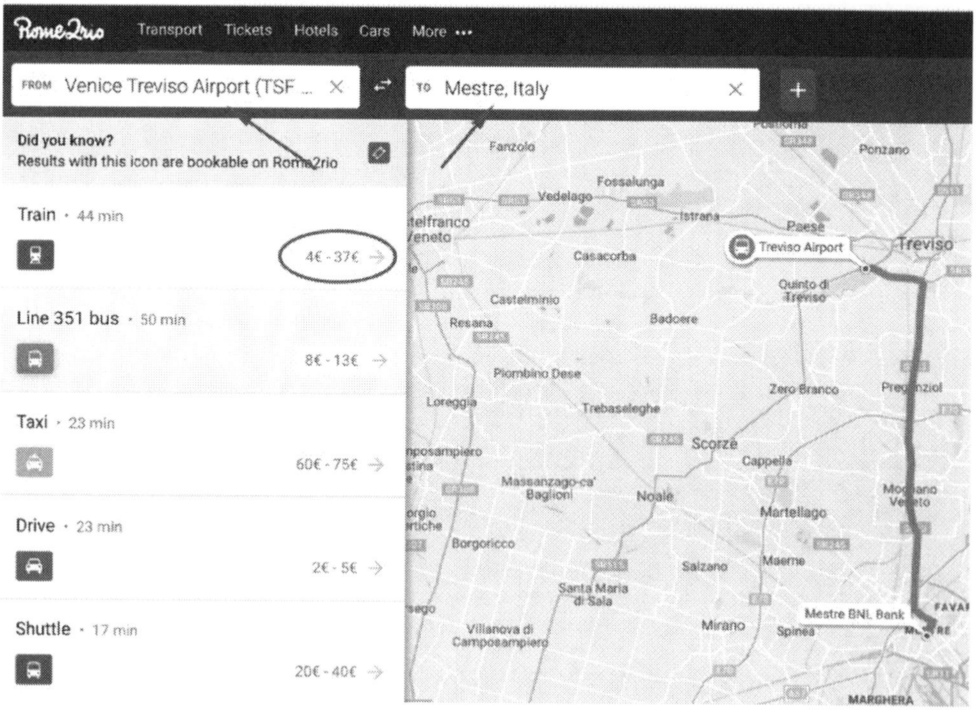

The service shows that the price of the train ride is €4 – 37. You need to go to the official Trenitalia website and see the current price there. There are no tickets with discounts available on February 1, but you can see what the usual price is for any other day. It turned out to be €7.05. And the travel time is 40 – 50 minutes.

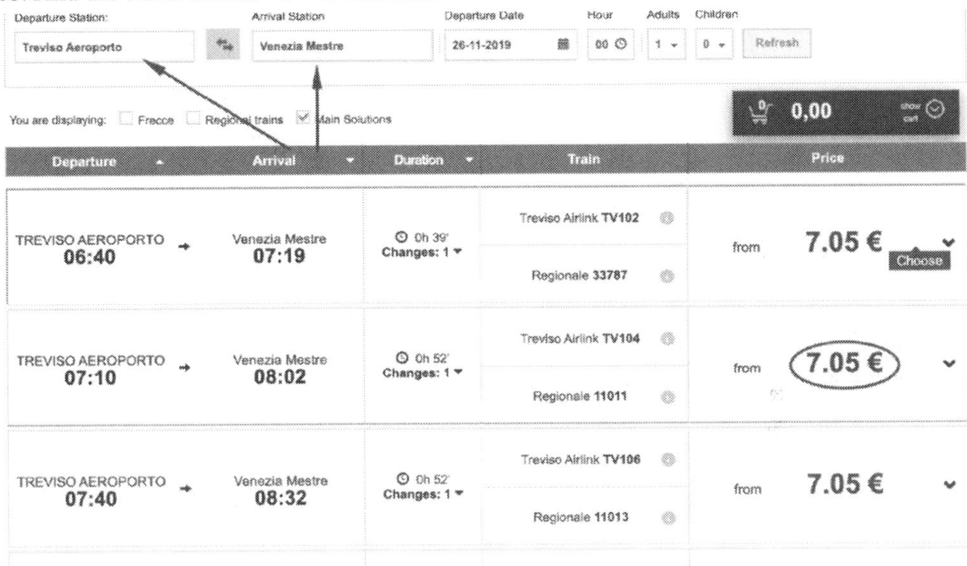

Now, let's add all this information to our table.

Start Date	End Date	Expense Item	Where From	Where To	Cost	Days
02.01.2020	02.01.2020	Flight	London	Venice Treviso	36	0
02.01.2020	02.01.2020	Train	Venice Treviso	Mestre	14	0
02.01.2020	02.09.2020	Apartment	Mestre	Mestre	303	8

By the way, the table must also include the cost of food, public transport, and sightseeing. Add another column called "Other Expenses" and fill it. Or instead, you can set some daily budget, such as €20. So, this is how the table should turn out.

Start Date	End Date	Expense Item	Where From	Where To	Cost	Other Expenses	Days
02.01.2020	02.01.2020	Flight	London	Venice Treviso	36	0	0
02.01.2020	02.01.2020	Train	Venice Treviso	Mestre	14	0	0
02.01.2020	02.09.2020	Apartment	Mestre	Mestre	303	160	8

Next, let's decide what city the couple will visit after Venice. There are several transport options that we can choose: a plane, a train, or a bus. To get started, let's choose the most convenient type of relocation — an airplane — and see how much it costs to fly from Venice to other cities in Italy.

From the list of Italian cities that I chose earlier, there is a good option for flying to only Naples on February 9, and it costs €17. Let's see more options on February 10. However, on this day, there is only one cheap flight to Naples, and it also costs €17.

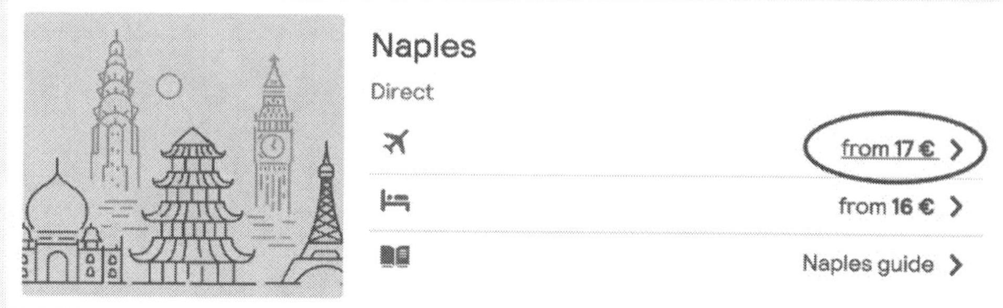

Now let's consider taking a bus or train. Geographically closer to Venice are Milan and Florence. Let's check them first.

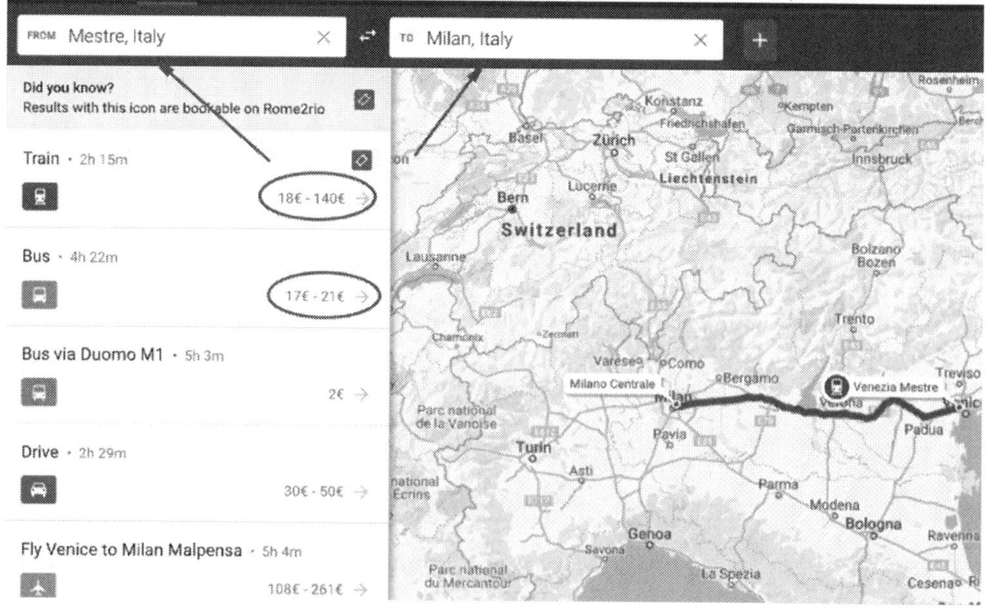

Rome2Rio shows that there is potentially a train from Mestre to Milan, which costs €18 and a bus for €17. We need to check whether this information is correct.

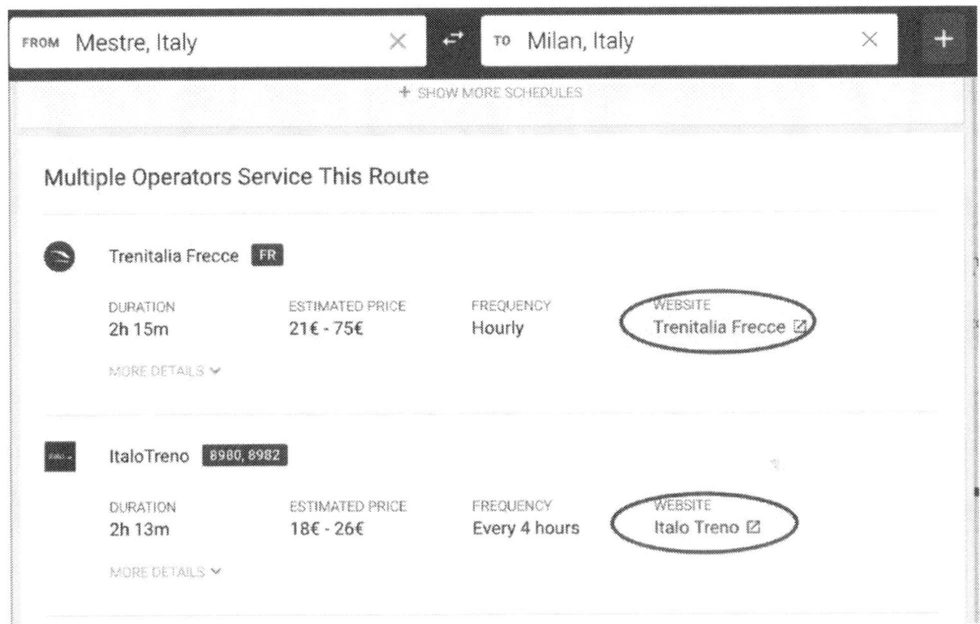

To check the train tickets, we need to go to the Trenitalia and Italo Treno websites. On the Trenitalia website, the cheapest ticket costs €20.

Departure		Arrival	Duration	Train		Price
Venezia Mestre 08:02 *	→	Milano Centrale 10:17	2h 15'	Frecciarossa 9712	from	27.90 €
Venezia Mestre 08:24 *	→	Milano Centrale 11:35	3h 11' Changes: 1	Regionale Veloce 2710 Regionale 2062	from	20.00 €
Venezia Mestre 08:32 *	→	Milano Centrale 10:45	2h 13'	Frecciarossa 1000 9714	from	27.90 €

The Italo Treno website shows that the most affordable option is €19.90. But the travel time is 1 hour shorter.

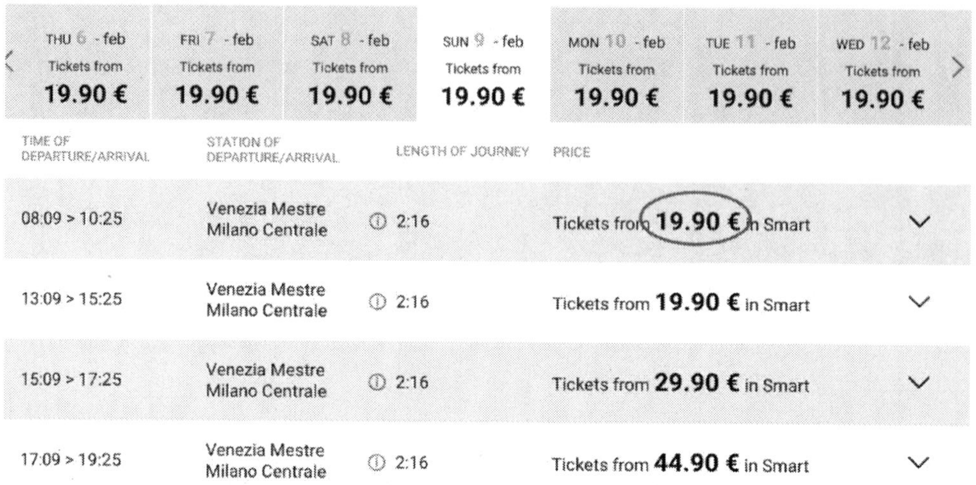

Besides, Italo Treno often holds sales and discounts of up to 50%. And now there is also such an offer. With the SERIE code, I received a discount and got a price of €13.90.

THU 6 - feb	FRI 7 - feb	SAT 8 - feb	SUN 9 - feb	MON 10 - feb	TUE 11 - feb	WED 12 - feb
Tickets from 13.90 €	Tickets from 13.90 €	Tickets from 13.90 €	Tickets from 13.90 €	Tickets from 13.90 €	Tickets from 13.90 €	Tickets from 13.90 €

TIME OF DEPARTURE/ARRIVAL	STATION OF DEPARTURE/ARRIVAL	LENGTH OF JOURNEY	PRICE
08:09 > 10:25	Venezia Mestre Milano Centrale	2:16	Tickets from 13.90 € in Smart
13:09 > 15:25	Venezia Mestre Milano Centrale	2:16	Tickets from 13.90 € in Smart
15:09 > 17:25	Venezia Mestre Milano Centrale	2:16	Tickets from 29.90 € in Smart

It remains to check the prices in other bus companies. Rome2Rio provides me such bus companies: Flixbus and MS.MK.

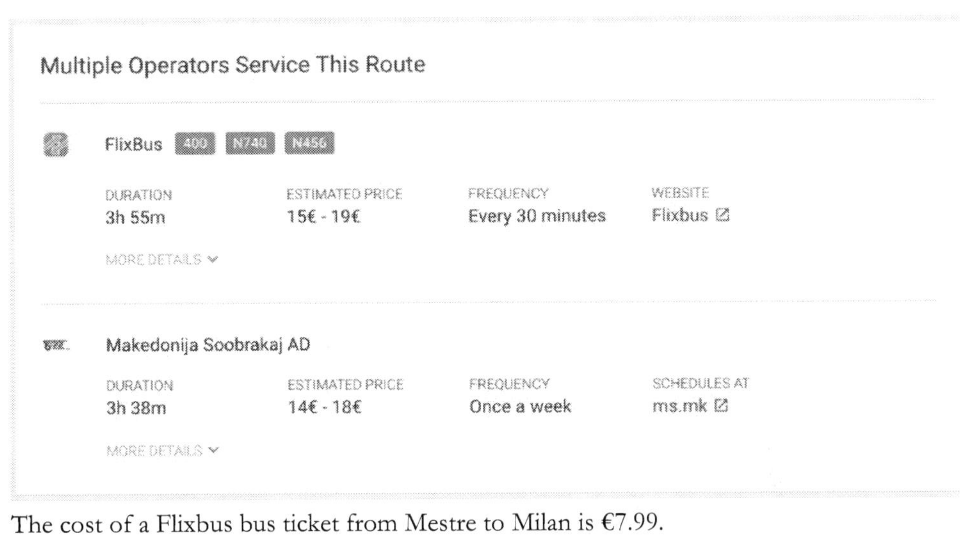

The cost of a Flixbus bus ticket from Mestre to Milan is €7.99.

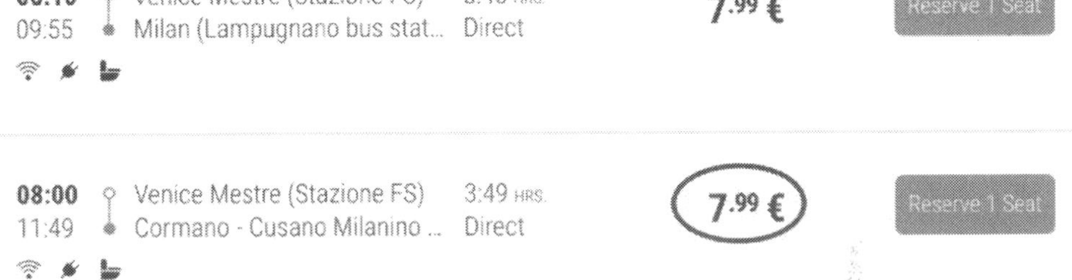

The MS.MK website, unfortunately, does not show the price, but it is unlikely that it is lower than that of Flixbus.

In the same way, we need to check the prices for the Mestre-Florence route. The bus and train companies are the same here: Flixbus, Trenitalia, and Italo Treno. And we found the following costs:

- Trenitalia – €19.90
- Italo Treno without a discount – €27.90, with a discount – €19.50
- Flixbus – €7.99

Let's also check the Mestre-Rome route. Here are the prices:

- Trenitalia – €25
- Italo Treno with a discount – €27.90
- Flixbus – €14.99

Now we need to choose a city that the couple will visit after Venice. We have the following options: by plane to Naples for €17 (but you need to take into account that there will be one more transfer to the airport, so that will cost extra), by bus to Milan for €7.99, to Florence for €8.99, or to Rome for €14.99.

To make a choice, it is important to understand from which city it is best to return to London at the end of February. Let's look at the ticket prices on February 29th. And the best option is Milan at €23.

Let's look up also February 28th. And again, Milan for €17. So Milan will be our final destination.

Now we should decide what city will be next after Venice: Florence, Naples, or Rome. If we take into account the price and time, Florence is better. But then it will be necessary to get from Florence to Rome, and then to Milan (since we agreed that the ideal option is four cities, Naples won't be among them).

So now we need to find out how much it will cost to get from Florence to Rome and from Rome to Milan. Let's look for tickets on February 16 and February 23.

Any Florence – Rome flight in February will cost €69 and higher.

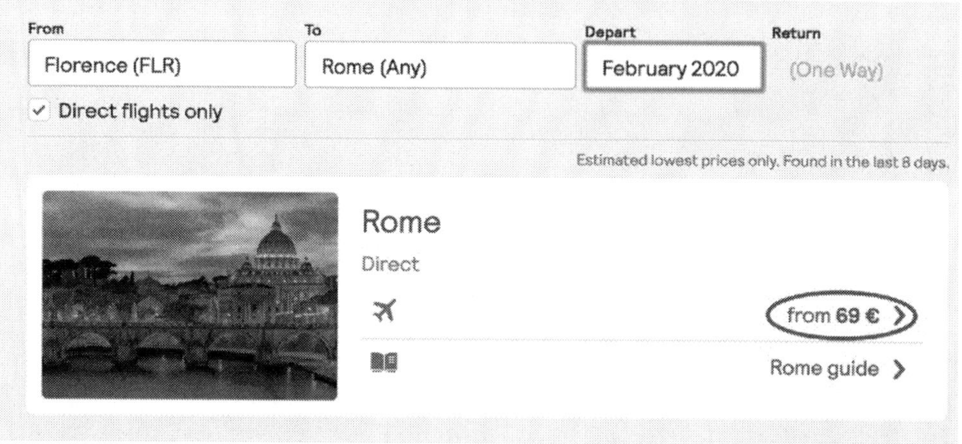

The Italo Treno train costs €13.90, and the Trenitalia train, €12.90.

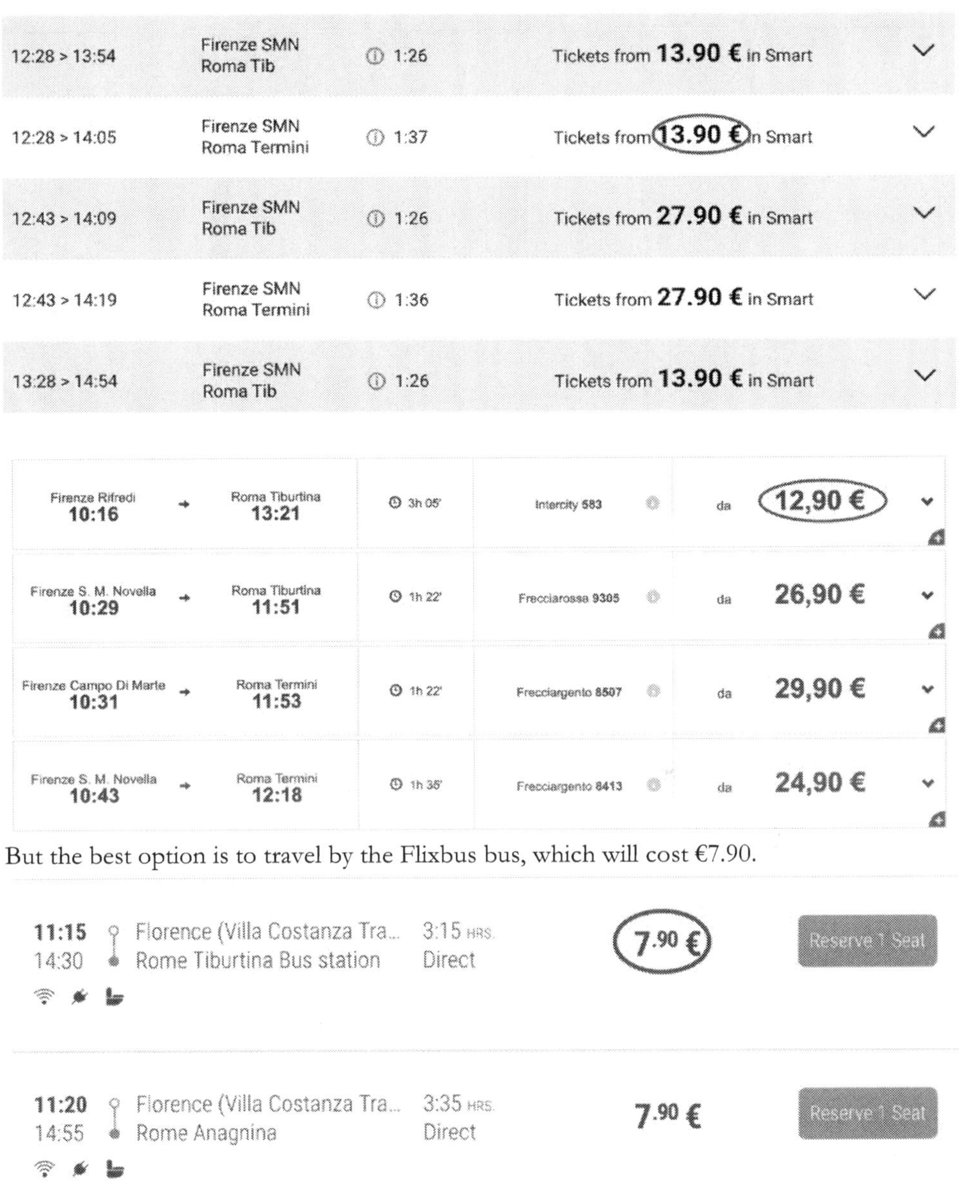

12:28 > 13:54	Firenze SMN Roma Tib	ⓘ 1:26	Tickets from **13.90 €** in Smart	∨
12:28 > 14:05	Firenze SMN Roma Termini	ⓘ 1:37	Tickets from **13.90 €** in Smart	∨
12:43 > 14:09	Firenze SMN Roma Tib	ⓘ 1:26	Tickets from **27.90 €** in Smart	∨
12:43 > 14:19	Firenze SMN Roma Termini	ⓘ 1:36	Tickets from **27.90 €** in Smart	∨
13:28 > 14:54	Firenze SMN Roma Tib	ⓘ 1:26	Tickets from **13.90 €** in Smart	∨

Departure		Arrival	Duration	Train		Price
Firenze Rifredi **10:16**	→	Roma Tiburtina **13:21**	3h 05'	Intercity 583	da	**12,90 €**
Firenze S. M. Novella **10:29**	→	Roma Tiburtina **11:51**	1h 22'	Frecciarossa 9305	da	**26,90 €**
Firenze Campo Di Marte **10:31**	→	Roma Termini **11:53**	1h 22'	Frecciargento 8507	da	**29,90 €**
Firenze S. M. Novella **10:43**	→	Roma Termini **12:18**	1h 35'	Frecciargento 8413	da	**24,90 €**

But the best option is to travel by the Flixbus bus, which will cost €7.90.

11:15 14:30	Florence (Villa Costanza Tra... Rome Tiburtina Bus station	3:15 HRS. Direct	7.90 €	Reserve 1 Seat
11:20 14:55	Florence (Villa Costanza Tra... Rome Anagnina	3:35 HRS. Direct	7.90 €	Reserve 1 Seat

Next, let's look at the prices for the Rome – Milan trip on February 23. Flight ticket costs €40 and higher.

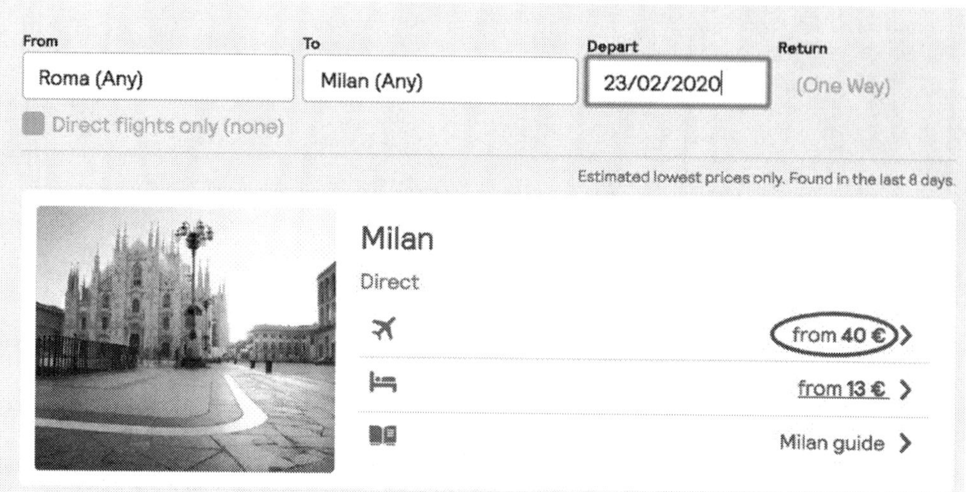

The train costs:

- Italo Treno – €31.40
- Trenitalia – €22.90

THU 6 - feb	FRI 7 - feb	SAT 8 - feb	SUN 9 - feb	MON 10 - feb	TUE 11 - feb	WED 12 - feb
Tickets from **31.40 €**	Tickets from **31.40 €**	Tickets from **31.40 €**	Tickets from **31.40 €**	Tickets from **31.40 €**	Tickets from **31.40 €**	Tickets from **31.40 €**

TIME OF DEPARTURE/ARRIVAL	STATION OF DEPARTURE/ARRIVAL	LENGTH OF JOURNEY	PRICE
05:40 > 09:08	Roma Termini Milano Rog	3:28	Tickets from **31.40 €** in Smart
05:40 > 09:20	Roma Termini Milano Centrale	3:40	Tickets from **31.40 €** in Smart
05:50 > 09:08	Roma Tib Milano Rog	3:18	Tickets from **31.40 €** in Smart

Partenza		Arrivo	Durata	Treno		Prezzo
Roma Termini 12:20	→	Milano Centrale 15:50	3h 30'	Frecciarossa 9528	da	47,50 €
Roma Termini 12:30	→	Milano Centrale 15:29	2h 59'	Frecciarossa 1000 9628	da	47,50 € Scegli
Roma Tiburtina 12:40	→	Milano Centrale 19:17	6h 37'	Intercity 590	da	22,90 €
Roma Termini 13:00	→	Milano Centrale 15:59	2h 59'	Frecciarossa 1000 9630	da	47,50 €
Roma Termini 13:12	→	Milano Centrale 21:53	8h 41' Cambi: 1	Regionale 23652 Intercity 684	da	24,25 €
Roma Termini 13:21	→	Milano Centrale 16:45	3h 24'	Frecciarossa 9532	da	47,50 €

The price of a Flixbus bus is €14.99. And this is again the optimal option, in my opinion.

08:30 17:00	Rome Tiburtina Bus station Milan (Lampugnano bus stat...	8:30 HRS. Direct	24.99 €	Reserve 1 Seat
09:25 17:50	Rome Tiburtina Bus station Milan (Lampugnano bus stat...	8:25 HRS. Direct	14.99 €	Reserve 1 Seat
09:30 19:05	Rome Tiburtina Bus station Milan (Lampugnano bus stat...	9:35 HRS. Direct	18.99 €	Reserve 1 Seat
09:40 19:09	Rome Tiburtina Bus station Cormano - Cusano Milanino ...	9:29 HRS. 1	23.98 €	Reserve 1 Seat
10:10 18:25	Rome Tiburtina Bus station Milan (Lampugnano bus stat...	8:15 HRS. Direct	14.99 €	Reserve 1 Seat

So, this is how the route through the cities of Italy looks: Venice – Florence – Rome – Milan

The next step will be to search for housing options in Florence, Rome, and Milan. I will search in the same way: first on Airbnb, and then I will check for cheaper options on Booking.

Let's look for an apartment in Florence for the following dates: February 9 – 16. The best option is a studio with a kitchen, Wi-Fi, and a 4.94 rating, which is very high. The price of this apartment is €298. It is worth noting that in Italy, you must pay a tourist tax (€42), regardless of the type of housing that you rent.

The next city is Rome. Let's look for an apartment for February 16 – 23. Since Rome is a rather large city, it is advisable to find housing in the city center, or if it is in the suburbs, then the cost should be significantly lower. The optimal price and location are the apartments in the very center of the city, which cost €220 for the entire stay.

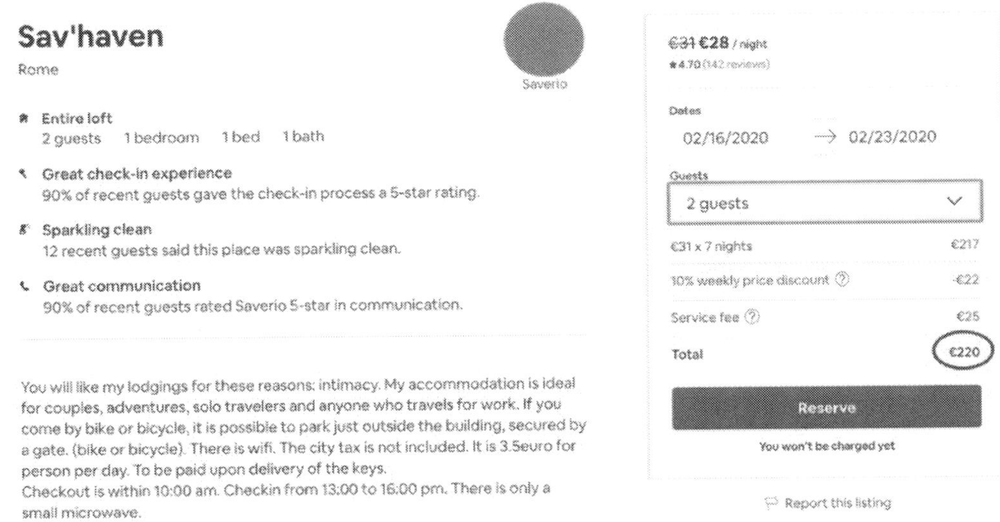

And finally, let's search for housing in Milan for February 23-28. The best suitable option for an apartment in the suburbs that costs €141. The center of Milan can be reached in 20 – 25 minutes, with a ticket price of €2.

Enter all the data in the table. For convenience, I recommend rounding off bus prices.

Start Date	End Date	Expense Item	Where From	Where To	Cost	Other Expenses	Days
02.01.2020	02.01.2020	Flight	London	Venice Treviso	36	0	0
02.01.2020	02.01.2020	Train	Venice Treviso	Mestre	14	0	0
02.01.2020	02.09.2020	Apartment	Mestre	Mestre	303	160	8
02.09.2020	02.09.2020	Bus	Mestre	Florence	18	0	0
02.09.2020	02.16.2020	Apartment	Florence	Florence	298	140	7
02.16.2020	02.16.2020	Bus	Florence	Rome	18	0	0
02.16.2020	02.23.2020	Apartment	Rome	Rome	220	140	7
02.23.2020	02.23.2020	Bus	Rome	Milan	30	0	0
02.23.2020	02.28.2020	Apartment	Milan	Milan	141	100	5

But this is not all. We still need to plan a transfer from Milan to the airport and the flight back to London (I remind you that on February 28, it costs €17). You can choose which airport you want to arrive at Southend or Gatwick. But the departure in both cases will be from Bergamo. From Milan to Bergamo airport, you can go cheaply and conveniently by the Terravision bus for only €6. It departs every half-hour.

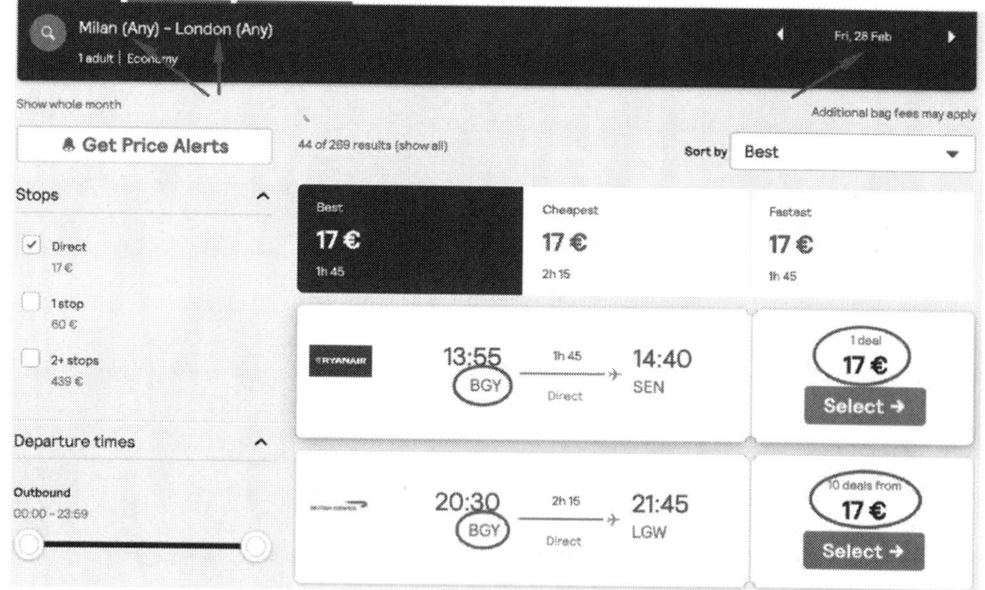

Outbound date: Wednesday 11 December 2019

MILAN CENTRAL STATION > BERGAMO AIRPORT

Departure time

00:00 arrives at 01:00 6.00 €	03:10 arrives at 04:10 6.00 €	03:30 arrives at 04:30 6.00 €	03:50 arrives at 04:50 6.00 €	04:30 arrives at 05:30 6.00 €
05:10 arrives at 06:10 6.00 €	05:40 arrives at 06:40 6.00 €	06:10 arrives at 07:10 6.00 €	06:40 arrives at 07:40 6.00 €	07:10 arrives at 08:10 6.00 €
07:40 arrives at 08:40 6.00 €	08:10 arrives at 09:10 6.00 €	08:40 arrives at 09:40 6.00 €	09:10 arrives at 10:10 6.00 €	09:40 arrives at 10:40 6.00 €

EARLIER

LATER

This is how your table with the route should look when you plan everything.

Start Date	End Date	Expense Item	Where From	Where To	Cost	Other Expenses	Days
02.01.2020	02.01.2020	Flight	London	Venice Treviso	36	0	0
02.01.2020	02.01.2020	Train	Venice Treviso	Mestre	14	0	0
02.01.2020	02.09.2020	Apartment	Mestre	Mestre	303	160	8
02.09.2020	02.09.2020	Bus	Mestre	Florence	18	0	0
02.09.2020	02.16.2020	Apartment	Florence	Florence	298	140	7
02.16.2020	02.16.2020	Bus	Florence	Rome	18	0	0
02.16.2020	02.23.2020	Apartment	Rome	Rome	220	140	7
02.23.2020	02.23.2020	Bus	Rome	Milan	30	0	0
02.23.2020	02.28.2020	Apartment	Milan	Milan	141	100	5
02.28.2020	02.28.2020	Bus	Milan	Milan Bergamo	12	0	0
02.28.2020	02.28.2020	Flight	Milan Bergamo	London	34	0	0
					1124	540	27

The trip will last 27 days. Thus, the couple needs €1124 for lodging and transport and €540 for food, public transport in cities, and sightseeing.

Let's also calculate how much money the couple will need to spend in 1 day. This number is especially helpful when comparing several routes with a different number of days. In our case, we get (€1124 + €540) ÷ 27 = €61.63. Below you can see how the complete table with the route will look.

A	B	C	D	E	F	G	H
Start Date	End Date	Expense Item	Where From	Where To	Cost	Other Expenses	Days
02.01.2020	02.01.2020	Flight	London	Venice Treviso	36	0	0
02.01.2020	02.01.2020	Train	Venice Treviso	Mestre	14	0	0
02.01.2020	02.09.2020	Apartment	Mestre	Mestre	303	160	8
02.09.2020	02.09.2020	Bus	Mestre	Florence	18	0	0
02.09.2020	02.16.2020	Apartment	Florence	Florence	298	140	7
02.16.2020	02.16.2020	Bus	Florence	Rome	18	0	0
02.16.2020	02.23.2020	Apartment	Rome	Rome	220	140	7
02.23.2020	02.23.2020	Bus	Rome	Milan	30	0	0
02.23.2020	02.28.2020	Apartment	Milan	Milan	141	100	5
02.28.2020	02.28.2020	Bus	Milan	Milan Bergamo	12	0	0
02.28.2020	02.28.2020	Flight	Milan Bergamo	London	34	0	0
					1124	540	27
							61.63

I note that this route was created based on my subjective preferences. You can rent a car, which means there will be no buses. You can separately count out the sum that will be spent on museum tickets and other attractions, or you can rent an apartment with a washing machine or a Jacuzzi.

You can also use the tricks that I wrote about earlier to save money: asking for a discount, cleaning the apartment by yourself, or trying to look for housing options without entering the dates. All of this influences the price and makes the trip cheaper.

So, we have planned the complete trip around Italy with Venice as the city that we begin with. Now I'll plan another trip, but with Venice at the end of it and the couple arriving not for the opening of the Carnival, but at its closing. I will not describe everything in such a detailed way, but just show you the complete route.

Start Date	End Date	Expense Item	Where From	Where To	Cost	Other Expenses	Days
02.01.2020	02.01.2020	Flight	London	Rome Chiampino	38	0	0
02.01.2020	02.01.2020	Train	Rome Chiampino	Rome	5	0	0
02.01.2020	02.08.2020	Apartment	Rome	Rome	230	140	7
02.08.2020	02.08.2020	Bus	Rome	Florence	16	0	0
02.08.2020	02.15.2020	Apartment	Florence	Florence	259	140	7
02.15.2020	02.15.2020	Bus	Florence	Milan	14	0	0
02.15.2020	02.21.2020	Apartment	Milan	Milan	170	120	6
02.21.2020	02.21.2020	Bus	Milan	Mestre	16	0	0
02.21.2020	02.28.2020	Apartment	Mestre	Mestre	313	140	7
02.28.2020	02.28.2020	Bus	Mestre	Venice Marco Polo	16	0	0
02.28.2020	02.28.2020	Flight	Venice Marco Polo	London	36	0	0
					1113	540	27
							61.22

The difference in price between the itinerary is insignificant. It is also possible to create a route with not four stops, but 5.

Start Date	End Date	Expense Item	Where From	Where To	Cost	Other Expenses	Days
02.01.2020	02.01.2020	Flight	London	Airport Naples	36	0	0
02.01.2020	02.01.2020	Bus	Airport Naples	Naples	2	0	0
02.01.2020	02.05.2020	Apartment	Naples	Naples	133	80	4
02.05.2020	02.05.2020	Bus	Naples	Rome	18	0	0
02.05.2020	02.12.2020	Apartment	Rome	Rome	220	140	7
02.12.2020	02.12.2020	Bus	Rome	Florence	16	0	0
02.12.2020	02.19.2020	Apartment	Florence	Florence	295	140	7
02.19.2020	02.19.2020	Bus	Florence	Mestre	18	0	0
02.19.2020	02.26.2020	Apartment	Mestre	Mestre	313	140	7
02.26.2020	02.26.2020	Bus	Mestre	Milan	16	0	0
02.26.2020	02.29.2020	Apartment	Milan	Milan	96	60	3
02.29.2020	02.29.2020	Bus	Milan	Milan Malpensa	12	0	0
02.29.2020	02.29.2020	Flight	Milan Malpensa	London	34	0	0
					1209	560	28
							63.18

As for me, this is the most interesting option. The trip will last one day longer, and the price will be almost €2 higher per day, compared to the second option. But the good thing is that thanks to this small change in price, we get the opportunity also to visit Naples.

Imagine that the couple also chose the third option. Now the trip is planned, and the next step will be to book everything.

The best time to book an apartment is as soon as possible, except when we book apartments during the peak of the season for a date that falls in the off-season period. This is due to the fact that during the peak of the season, the apartment owners put the highest prices, and they often remain the same for several months or even six months, which is why apartments can turn out to be overpriced. And when the peak of the season has passed, they place a lower price. But this is not our case. Therefore, it is better to book lodging as early as possible.

It is also better to book the train and bus tickets in advance. But if you wait, there is a chance to get on some a limited-time special offer and buy them with a discount.

It is advisable to book flights somewhere 2 – 3 months before the trip. Airlines often offer discounts a few months before the flight date. Therefore, if you book earlier, the price will be higher, and if you wait too long, it may turn out that there are no cheap tickets specifically for your dates.

To keep you from getting confused, I marked in the table everything that I have already booked and paid for in green. If I buy something at a different price (as in not one that was in the original table), then I change the price in the table and again highlight it green. Thus, you will quickly understand what has not yet been bought and how much money is needed for it. Here is an example of a table when you have already paid for lodging.

Start Date	End Date	Expense Item	Where From	Where To	Cost	Other Expenses	Days
02.01.2020	02.01.2020	Flight	London	Airport Naples	36	0	0
02.01.2020	02.01.2020	Bus	Airport Naples	Naples	2	0	0
02.01.2020	02.05.2020	Apartment	Naples	Naples	133	80	4
02.05.2020	02.05.2020	Bus	Naples	Rome	18	0	0
02.05.2020	02.12.2020	Apartment	Rome	Rome	220	140	7
02.12.2020	02.12.2020	Bus	Rome	Florence	16	0	0
02.12.2020	02.19.2020	Apartment	Florence	Florence	295	140	7
02.19.2020	02.19.2020	Bus	Florence	Mestre	18	0	0
02.19.2020	02.26.2020	Apartment	Mestre	Mestre	313	140	7
02.26.2020	02.26.2020	Bus	Mestre	Milan	16	0	0
02.26.2020	02.29.2020	Apartment	Milan	Milan	96	60	3
02.29.2020	02.29.2020	Bus	Milan	Milan Malpensa	12	0	0
02.29.2020	02.29.2020	Flight	Milan Malpensa	London	34	0	0
					1209	560	28
							63.18

This way looks at the process of finding the best travel route. The more practice you have, the less time it will take to plan your dream trip. For example, it takes me about 20 – 30 minutes to create such a small route.

Conclusion

While creating this book, I tried my best to use more visual information, which includes many screenshots. And on the contrary, I didn't provide much general and public information that can you find on almost every website or any other travel book. It may be that my advice and ways of travel planning are not suitable for everyone, because there are things that I described very subjectively. But still, I hope that this book will prove to be useful to you.

And also I would like to ask - if you want to give a negative review, think of such a thing — using at least one of the many tips that I have provided in this book, you will already save at least a couple of times more than you spent on this book.

Appendix 1. Low-Cost Airlines

Air Arabia: a low-cost airline with a hub in Sharjah. It carries out flights in Asia, Africa, and Eastern Europe.

Air Asia: one of the best low-cost airlines in the world. The central hub is located in Kuala Lumpur. It has a massive route network throughout Asia and Australia.

Air Cairo: an EgyptAir subsidiary low-cost airline. It flies from the main cities of Egypt to Europe.

Air Canada Rouge: a subsidiary low-cost airline of the national carrier Air Canada. It offers many flights to Europe.

Air Transat: a low-cost airline based in Montreal. It operates domestic flights in Canada and the USA, flights to Europe in the summer, and flights to the Caribbean and Central America in the winter.

Azul: a Brazilian low-cost airline with a large number of domestic destinations, as well as flights to Argentina, the USA, and Portugal.

Cebu Pacific: a Philippine low-cost airline with many domestic flights. It also flies throughout East and Southeast Asia and to Australia.

China United: a Chinese low-cost airline with a hub in Beijing and domestic flights that cost $10 and higher one-way.

Condor: another subsidiary of Lufthansa. It is a charter airline that carries out flights in exotic countries: South and North America, the Caribbean, Africa, and Asia.

EasyJet: a low-cost airline that operates flights mainly in the Western European countries and has many flights departing from the U.K.

EuroWings: a subsidiary of Lufthansa. It operates flights in Europe, the USA, and Asia, as well as the Caribbean.

Fastjet: a whole group of African low-cost airlines. It operates flights in Zimbabwe, Mozambique, South Africa, and Zambia.

Flair Airlines: a low-cost airline based in Edmonton and Winnipeg. It operates flights to other cities of Canada and the USA.

Fly Frontier: an American low-cost airline with a hub in Denver. It operates flights around the U.S., as well as ones to Canada, Mexico, and the Dominican Republic.

FlyDubai: an airline with a base in Dubai. It has reasonable ticket prices for long flights across Africa and Asia. There are also flights to European cities.

GOL: one more airline with a hub in Brazil. It operates many international flights. The domestic flights cost less than the ones operated by Azul.

InterJet: in comparison with other Mexican low-cost airlines, it offers more international destinations — - flights to Cuba, Peru, Colombia, and Canada.

Jeju Air: the main low-cost airline in South Korea. It carries out many domestic flights, also as well as flights to countries in Southeast Asia and the Far East.

JetBlue: an American low-cost airline based in New York. It offers flights around the USA, as well as to Mexico, the Caribbean, Ecuador, Colombia, and Peru.

JetStar: a subsidiary of the Australian company Qantas, based in Melbourne. It operates flights in Australia, New Zealand, and the countries of Southeast Asia.

Jin Air: a subsidiary airline of Korean Air. It offers flights throughout the region, as well as to Hawaii, Australia, and Guam.

Juneyao Airlines: a large airline with a base in Shanghai. It has a flight network in China, and also operates flights to Japan, South Korea, and Thailand.

LATAM Argentina: a low-cost airline based in Argentina, is a part of the LATAM Airlines Group. It operates domestic flights in Argentina, as well as in Brazil, Peru, Chile, and the United States.

Laudamotion: a subsidiary of Ryanair which operates flights to Europe. It often creates discounts with €0.99 – - €5 tickets.

LEVEL: a subsidiary of British Airways and Iberia. It carries out flights from Spanish and French cities to Canada, the USA, and Latin America. Prices for transatlantic one-way flights start from €90.

Nok Air: a Thai low-cost airline is operating domestic flights and flights to other countries in the region.

Norwegian Air: a Norwegian low-cost airline that operates within Europe, and also carries out flights to the United States, South America, and Asia. It provides services of very high quality, therefore, their price is slightly higher than that of other European low-cost airlines.

Pegasus: a Turkish airline with a hub in Istanbul. It is a suitable option for booking cheap tickets to Turkey since most European low-cost airlines do not fly there.

Pobeda: a subsidiary low-cost airline of the Russian airline Aeroflot. It now has more than 50 destinations.

Ryanair: a very popular low-cost airline in Europe and even all over the world. It operates flights in Europe and some countries in Africa. The airline creates discounts several times a month.

Sky Airline: a Chilean low-cost airline. It operates domestic flights, as well as flights to Peru, Bolivia, Argentina, Brazil, and Uruguay. Prices for one-way flights start at $10.

Solaseed Air: a Japanese low-cost airline that has discounts for foreign tourists.

Southwest Airlines: one of the first American low-cost companies. The airline routes are concentrated in the United States, but it also operates flights to Central America and the Caribbean.

Spirit: the routes are about the same as JetBlue's. Prices are slightly lower, but there are not so many flights.

Spring Airlines: a Chinese low-cost airline with a base in Shanghai. It carries out flights in China and neighboring countries. The prices start at $15 for a one-way ticket.

Sun Country: a low-cost airline with a standard set of routes for the USA — - domestic flights, Central America, the Caribbean.

Sunwing Airlines: a subsidiary of the Sunwing Travel Group. It operates flights from Canadian cities to the United States, the Caribbean, and Central America.

Thai Lion Air: a Thai subsidiary low-cost airline of the Indonesian airline Lion Air Group. In addition to domestic flights to Thailand, there are flights to China and other cities in the region.

Tiger Air and Scoot: since 2017, it can be considered as one company. It is a Singapore Airlines subsidiary low-cost airline. It carries out flights in Asia and Australia, plus flights to Berlin, Athens, and Hawaii.

Transavia: a low-cost airline of the Air France-KLM parent company. It provides flights mainly to southern Europe and northern Africa.

Vanilla Air: a subsidiary airline of the All Nippon Airways. It operates flights Flights among the cities of Japan, as well as to Hong Kong and Taiwan.

Virgin Australia: a low-cost company of the Virgin Group. It has four bases in Australia, operates flights in Oceania, Indonesia, Hong Kong, and the United States.

Viva Aerobus: a Mexican low-cost airline jointly founded by IAMSA and Ryanair. It operates flights to Mexico, the United States, and Costa Rica.

Volaris: a low-cost airline based in Mexico City, Guadalajara, and Tijuana. It operates domestic flights in Mexico, but there are also flights to the USA, El Salvador, Costa Rica, and Guatemala.

Volotea: a Spanish low-cost airline with hubs in Spain, France, and Italy. Most flights are operated in the Mediterranean. It often carries out discounts with tickets for €1 for members of the Megavolotea program.

Vueling: a Spanish airline based in Barcelona. It operates various flights both in Spain and in European countries.

WestJet: a Canadian low-cost airline with hubs in Toronto, Calgary, and Vancouver. It operates flights in North America and the Caribbean and Europe.

Wizz Air: a major European low-cost airline. Most hubs are located in Eastern Europe. If you plan to fly Wizz Air more than once a year, it's best to buy a membership in the Wizz Air Discount Club.

Appendix 2. Low-Cost Bus Companies

Ecolines: a cheap bus network is covering 21 countries and about 200 cities, most of which are located in Central and Eastern Europe.

Eurolines: one of the largest European bus carriers. It operates in almost all European countries. Lifehack: there is a special offer available called the Eurolines Pass — pay €195 and get an unlimited ticket for 15 days.

Flibco: a bus company that carries out low-cost transfers to airports in Europe (Brussel Charleroi, Frankfurt Hahn, Porto, Tenerife). The first ticket for any direction costs €5.

FlixBus: the youngest and most progressive European bus company. It operates in more than 1000 cities and 27 countries. They also began to work in the U.S. and the U.K. The company often carries out discounts, including a €0.99 discount per one-way tickets.

Greyhound: the largest bus company in the USA operating in all major cities and tourist sites of the USA and Canada. The company owns 16,000 thousand buses that depart daily in 3,100 directions. They also maintain partnerships with other bus companies.

Lux Express: a large bus company that focuses more on Eastern Europe. It has a subsidiary low-cost bus carrier, Simple Express, on which the first five tickets cost only €3.

MegaBus: a bus company with almost free tickets that operates in Europe, the U.K., Canada, and the USA.

Regiojet: a Czech bus company that operates more in Central Europe. It has an especially extensive route network in the Czech Republic and Slovakia.

Appendix 3. Travel Resources

Accuweather: a weather forecast site. It has a user-friendly interface and many viewing options: hourly, daily, monthly.

Agoda: a service very similar to Booking, but. The only difference is that it has a lot more options in Asia.

Airbnb: a website where you can find announcements from individuals who- owners of apartments and houses. The site probably has the most significant number of apartments for booking, and the prices here are lower than in similar services and hotels.

Blablacar: a service that brings together drivers and companions around the world. The service itself is free, but drivers charge money for the trip. It is important to remember that this is not the same as hitchhiking.

Booking: the largest search website for hotel and hostel bookings. It has the largest database of options. This service is especially useful if you plan a trip to Europe, North and Latin America, and Australia.

Couchsurfing: a website where you can find free housing and great company in an unfamiliar city.

Fly4free: a website where you can find cheap flight options, apartments, and hotels, cruises, etc. It has convenient navigation, as well as the ability to track suitable offers by country and continent.

Foursquare: a resource that positions itself as a city guide, but I often use it to find places where you can eat tasty and inexpensive food.

Holidaypirates: it is similar to the previous resource, but in my opinion, contains less options and more ready-made routes.

Momondo: an international travel website that is similar in functionality to Skyscanner.

Nomadlist: a website for choosing a country to travel or relocate to. It contains many characteristics for assessing the quality of life of a country or city and comparing them with each other.

Rome2rio: a chic service that shows by what means of transport you can be able to get from one point to another. The only disadvantage is that the prices on it are not always correct and must be checked manually.

Secretflying: a service that allows you to search for the best deals on flights.

Skyscanner: in my opinion, this is the best ticket search service. It has wide functionality that allows you to find the cheapest tickets in various ways.

Tripit: a service that allows you to store all documents in one place — - electronic checks, tickets, bookings, policies, and scans of documents. Also, Tripit shows the weather, maps, and entertainment programs for the destination city, and makes it possible to book tickets to theaters and reserve tables in restaurants.

Uber: a service for getting a ride and finding passengers. You can call and pay for taxis or private drivers. The application is available almost all over the world.

About the Author

My name is George Laas. I am 33 years old, and traveling is my hobby. I started traveling relatively recently — my first trip abroad was when I turned 28. During these five years, I have visited 42 countries and 118 cities. Usually, I travel 4 – 5 times a year, and during every trip, I visit several countries. Besides, I always build my route in such a way that I get to visit a couple of cities in each country and see as many exciting places as possible.

At first, I traveled alone, then with my wife, and for the last two years, I have been planning trips for my friends and acquaintances, who encouraged me to write this book and share my experience with other people.